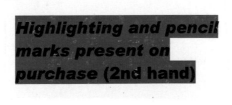

On the Wires
of Our Nerves

On the Wires of Our Nerves

The Art of Electroacoustic Music

EDITED BY

Robin Julian Heifetz

Lewisburg
Bucknell University Press
London and Toronto: Associated University Presses

Associated University Presses
440 Forsgate Drive
Cranbury, NJ 08512

Associated University Presses
25 Sicilian Avenue
London WC1A 2QH, England

Associated University Presses
P.O. Box 488, Port Credit
Mississauga, Ontario
Canada L5G 4M2

The paper used in this publication meets the requirements
of the American National Standard for permanence of Paper
for Printed Library Materials Z39.48-1984.

Library of Congress Cataloging-in-Publication Data

On the wires of our nerves.

  Bibliography: p.
  Discography: p.
  1. Computer music—History and criticism.
2. Electronic music—History and criticism.   3. Computer composition.   I. Heifetz, Robin Julian, 1951–
ML1380.05   1989   789.9'9   87-46435
ISBN 0-8387-5155-5 (alk. paper)

PRINTED IN THE UNITED STATES OF AMERICA

For Lucien Goethals

As soon as a person wishes to bring about something which to the best of his knowledge would never happen without him, he embarks on a process of creation. If, in addition to that, his interest lies in putting things together—establishing connections between things—that otherwise would not connect by themselves, and if he then connects them in such a way that they have a meaning and sense that without these connections they would not have, then he is a composer.

—Herbert Brün

Contents

8

On the Wires
of Our Nerves

Introduction

Robin Julian Heifetz

The fundamental social function of any compositional idea must be that of communication.[1] Composers must ask themselves: first, what are the inherent properties of the compositional idea such that it requires disclosure at all? In other words, does the idea evince a heartfelt and vivid impression, does it convince the listener by virtue of its unencumbered and incisive presentation, or does it manifest a substantial, enduring character? Second, if the music appears valid, then the responsible composer must ask what are its inherent properties such that it requires expression in any of the electroacoustic media above all other musical or nonmusical creative media? What can any of these media achieve for the composer vis-à-vis communication that expression in the other media cannot possibly realize? Ostensibly, involvement in any of these media owing to the mere discovery or desire to present strikingly new timbral qualities and abstractions is not justifiable; the compositional concept must be worthy of the medium.

Certainly, music is but one method of discourse. It is, however, far more significant a means of communication in nonliterate cultures where it is of an immediate and practical utility. In addition, the individual here is not a specialist in composition. All members in a given cultural framework usually take part in the act of musical creativity, which cannot be clearly delineated from other aspects of tribal life, serving as essential aids to agriculture, medicine, religion, and ritualistic-magical activity. All of these elements are closely intertwined and complement one another.

In our society, however, we have witnessed the evolution of the composer as a specialist. In the postwar era a schism developed between the composer, the listener, and other musical practitioners as compositional intricacy gradually expanded. The resultant social differentiation has produced enclaves in which radically

11

new and innovative forms of creativity have become a very significant, if not the only, standard of judgment among one's peers.

By extension, electroacoustic composers have isolated themselves even further from their audience and its critical needs. They have been hiding behind masks for far too long. The electroacoustic media have served as a haven for experimentalists who have ceased to gauge their artistic visions according to the exigencies and aesthetics of their society. As Jean-Baptiste Barrière of IRCAM has made known rather passionately:

> If this community does not react, and does not become conscious of its responsibilities, it will condemn itself in the short term, instead of building itself up as the competent and rigorous interlocutor that it could be if it chose to play a useful role for all musicians. The community must be able to take care of its memory, to guarantee an accumulation of knowledge that never loses track of its real objective: music. To do useful work and then justify it, it must be a transmission structure for knowledge and information, it must help to validate them, and it must be done with and in the service of musicians, and not of a minority of opportunists [technologists] who take advantage of a temporary situation of ignorance.[2]

This suggests aspirations toward, and an appreciation of, higher aesthetic ideals that have thus far not been demonstrated very often in a musical world rife with technology.

That is exactly what this anthology is all about. But any changes must come about slowly and painstakingly as a consequence of a reexamination of these important sociocultural values. The essays I have selected will hopefully kindle the reader's interest in these models of artistic workmanship and essential communication.

In part 1, Leonard Kasdan and Jon H. Appleton discuss the impact of modernization and its effect upon our musical culture. They call attention to the revolutionizing of our traditional conceptions of music and how electroacoustic music may be viewed as an extrapolation of western technology and intellectual developments. Otto Luening's essay presents a sketch of electroacoustic music and its profound effect on twentieth-century music practices. Daria Semegen explores the composer's real link with the world and proposes that appreciation of other art forms can enrich the composer's aesthetic sensibilities and working methods. Significant constraints remain despite the fact that electroacoustic music was initially viewed by composers as a form of musical liberation; both Kenneth Gaburo's and David Keane's articles formulate questions on constraints the composer derives from psychoacoustic and structural/functional conditions for perception. Jan W. Morthenson focuses on the aesthetic dilemmas of the absence of natural references as well as that of relating foreground and background elements. He maintains that electroacoustic music has one basic characteristic: its dependence on external elements, both as references and as subjects. The purpose of Jon H. Appleton's paper is to demonstrate that aesthetic and scientific considerations can be separated, and he outlines some fundamental aesthetic criteria both for study and composition. Barry Schrader's essay focuses on the meanings of "style," offers some definitions, and examines how composers develop personal characteristics in their music.

In part 2, my article amplifies the problems of computer technology versus artistry and the composer's responsibility to touch the audience. I recommend a new social dynamic in which both composer and listener take each other into account as equal participants in an act of communication. John Melby discusses problems posed for the composer in a field that has come to be dominated by technicians rather than by those trained in the art of musical composition. David Keane's essay similarly suggests that we must rediscover strategies that appeal to the working of the human mind rather than those which merely derive from the workings of our computers. Thomas E. Janzen's article focuses on computer-assisted composition software that could permit specification of scores in aesthetic terms, such as appeals to recognition, historical memory, and beauty instead of merely as frequencies and envelopes.

In part 3, Lejaren Hiller analyzes his fifty-three minute tape work, *Electronic Sonata,* written in sonata form and combining endlessly repeating glissandi with environmental sounds that he subjects to many combinations and metamorphoses. Herbert Brün's article aggressively invites reconsideration of the roles played by aesthetics, social and political thinking, self-reference, commercial realism, and all so-called musical theory while talking about a number of his compositions. The concept of imago-abstract sound began as an integral part to musique concrète; Priscilla McClean provides an analysis of her imago-abstract sound work *Dance of Dawn* and discusses the ability of such sound structures to generate unity and coherence while evoking several simultaneous auditory responses. Jon H. Appleton's examination of his maturation as a composer culminates in an in-depth study of his work *'Otahiti,* which incorporates indigenous Polynesian elements. Dexter Morrill's paper is concerned with practical problems both composers and performers encounter in mixed media. He speaks about several of his works that gave rise to these observations and proposes a compositional strategy that will take advantage of the new musical "instrument" known as the loudspeaker.

Notes

1. José Maria Neves, "Education by and for Electroacoustic Music: Topics for Reflection," *FAIRE 4/5: Journées d'Étude Internationale des Musiques Electroacoustiques,* trans. J. Chopin, 4, no. 5, 1975, p. 37.

2. Jean-Baptiste Barrière, "The Music: Essays on the 1986 International Computer Music Conference," *Computer Music Journal* 11, no. 2 (Summer 1987): 37–38.

Part 1

Overview: Considerations and Problems in the Creative Decision-making Process

Tradition and Change:
The Case of Music

Leonard Kasdan
DALHOUSIE UNIVERSITY

Jon H. Appleton
DARTMOUTH COLLEGE

The cultural patterning of perceptions has long been an accepted fact. The ways we see and hear are learned. Special institutional mechanisms that serve to perpetuate such traditional patterns exist in all societies and have recently received attention by those interested in their transformation through modernization. Thus in order to study "The Primitive World and Its Transformation," Robert Redfield felt it necessary to focus upon what he called "the social organization of tradition."[1] He placed major emphasis upon those institutions that traditionally had perpetuated and elaborated the great philosophical and religious traditions of ancient civilizations while keeping them integrated with the little traditions of peasant villagers. This was accomplished through drawing upon the creative impulses of the little tradition as sources of new stimuli to serve as points of departure for further elaboration of the great tradition. These would reinfluence the little tradition, establishing a chain of mutual interdependence.

The impact of modernization has served radically to alter the role of tradition in many societies. In particular, the impact of modern science and technology has greatly weakened the position of systems of belief, perception, and social organization of tradition. This transformation has become a major area of interest for students in many disciplines. Whether studying economic changes, political changes, or changes in world view, all have had to take into account major alterations in traditional culture patterns under the impact of a transformation by the West. This has been true whether the student concentrated upon those aspects which are the result of the impact of western ideas or those which are reactions to the introduction of western technology.

As a result of the study of the transformation of traditional society, there has developed a dichotomy between modern and traditional societies that has treated the modern (western) as a largely finished entity to which traditional society could be compared. This has had great heuristic value in helping us to understand change in traditional societies, but it has had the less fortunate consequence of leading us to neglect quite radical transformations of traditional patterns still existing in "modern societies." This paper seeks to call attention to one such transformation in modern western societies—a transformation that is revolutionizing traditional conceptions of music as well as the role of the performer, composer, and audience. This change, like many others in traditional society, is being accomplished through the impact of rapid technological innovation.

The focus upon this transformation in the field of music is a particularly instructive one, for the relationships of great and little musical traditions are widespread, and there is no difficulty in defining musical behavior or the status of "musician" in terms of nearly universal applicability. In addition, musician status and the settings within which musical behavior occurs are easier to define and isolate for purposes of analysis than activities such as "philosophizing."

Traditional music, once it has passed beyond the level at which every member of the society is his own composer, performer, and instrument maker, soon develops special statuses of "musician" that recognize special skill, ability, and training. Once this occurs there is the additional possibility of a bifurcation as particular types of music and performance, confined to exotic settings of differentiated and stratified societies, are developed. Thus the development of liturgical music, confined to sacred settings, or court music, confined to an equally restricted setting, leads to specialized relationships between musicians and patrons distinct from the status relations and settings that characterize "folk" music. This is true despite the fact that liturgical and court music frequently use folk themes as a basis for elaboration. The distinction is a commonplace one in the history of all complex societies regardless of the diverse influences of varied cultural traditions. Thus there is no difficulty in applying the western dichotomy of folk-classical to the Indian subcontinent, the Arab world, Japan, China, or Bali, etc.

At the classical end of the spectrum, set pieces or compositions soon become part of a well-established repertory in the West, as in other traditions. The West was unique, however, in developing a system of musical notation that more and more permitted a set of instructions to narrowly specify the manner in which a piece was to be performed. In contrast, the notations developed by non-western classical traditions, to the extent that they are present at all (there are none beyond those which at most indicate broad patterns in classical Indian or Indonesian music) are much looser, leaving enormously greater leeway for variation on the part of the performer. William P. Malm, in discussing the Gagakû notational system, points out that

> The Japanese system is further complicated by the fact that most of the characteristic melismas are learned while memorizing the solfège so that they seldom are apparent to the eye. In addition, the words of the solfège do not stand for definite pitches or are only a few evolutionary steps above "la-de-da" singing as far as accuracy is concerned.[2]

The consequence of this difference is enormously important for understanding the history and present trends in western music.

When Roger Sessions delivered a series of six lectures at the Juilliard School of Music in 1949, he offered one of the first concise descriptions of the way in which western culture had divided the previously unitary role of the composer-performer into *three* distinct activities, those of performer, composer, listener.[3] Briefly stated, Sessions concerned himself with the initial split between those who listened and those who made music. The relatively sophisticated division between composer and the performer within the later group is largely a creation of western culture,[4] since in an improvisatory tradition such a distinction does not exist.

As western music became more complex, the role of improvisation greatly diminished. The several syntaxes of western music make it impossible for the performer to convey large quantities of new information to the listener unless the composition is completely random or the improvisation has been carefully structured before the performance. Such structuring of music placed greater demands on the performer and increased the difficulty of accu-

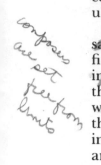

rate re-creation. This is one explanation for the increased social importance of the performer and the creation of the nineteenth-century virtuoso. However, the roles of performer and composer ultimately became extremely difficult to execute simultaneously.

With the rise of the virtuoso performer, the composer was saddled with a burden, which, in the last twenty years, he has finally found a way to cast off. As the performer's role grew in importance, flagrant neglect of the score became the rule rather than the exception, and as a consequence the composer felt that it was more difficult than ever to reach his audience. Composers in the first half of this century cluttered their scores with instructions in the hope that performers would be able to recreate the subtlety and complexity of their work. The performer was often so frightened by the new demands placed on him that he devoted the majority of his programs to the music of preceding centuries.

Virtuosity is certainly stressed in nonwestern classic traditions, but the context in which it occurs is radically different from that just described. Composition is largely the result of virtuoso performance. A musician in the course of performance improvises new forms, which strike the imagination of the performer himself and of other musicians, who then seize upon them as the basis for further elaboration, largely of an improvisatory nature. Thus the highly sophisticated performance of, for example, a Ravi Shankar in Indian music is not pure improvisation but is based upon traditionally given forms (ragas). The performance is evaluated according to the performer's ability to improvise within a given framework. In fact, any performer who developed a standardized interpretation would be judged a failure as a musician regardless of his skill.

This generalization must be modified to account for cases where the nature of instrumentation combined with ensemble playing precludes the kinds of improvisation we have been discussing. Thus McPhee writes with regard to Balinese music:

I have often been asked if, with no musical notation before them, Balinese musicians ever play a piece the same way twice. Is their performance not essentially improvised? This shows a complete misunderstanding of gamelan organization. Other than in solo parts there can be no place for spontaneous improvisation where all component parts are doubled by two, four, six, or more instruments. Unison in the different parts must prevail or utter confusion results. While different gamelans may play the same composition differently, each must always play its own version as learned as rehearsal. This, of course, does not mean that all performances are note perfect. Individual mistakes occur from time to time but the main line is firmly held by the ensemble as a whole.

In considering the musical examples, a distinction should be made between solo and unison passages. The solo is never the final melodic version, for here the performer is free to take certain liberties in the way of embellishing tones or retarding a melodic tone. The unison passage, on the other hand, has concrete finality. It is something worked out. It exists in the minds of the musicians as clearly as though it were read from a printed page. Like the composition itself, it can only be changed at rehearsal, when some other pattern may be substituted.[5]

The lack of notation in a situation that severely restricts improvisation makes the learning of a new piece a much more involved process than in those traditions where a notation is present.

New compositions are learned from a teacher through melodic dictation, phrase by phrase, with each phrase repeated until a complete melodic section has been memorized. The ornamental parts are patiently worked out in the same way. Learning a new composition may take the group a month. Only after another month of practice will the music really begin to flow. The ease and rhythmic precision desired by all before playing the piece in public may not be reached before several months have passed. Music to accompany dramatic choreographies such as legong presents further problems and may take even longer before the perfect coordination of phrase, accents, and tempo changes with the gestures and movements of the dancers has been attained.[6]

Thus the distinction between two traditions holds even when they share a nonimprovisatory ensemble tradition.

Biological evolution presents striking analogies. The history of music before these latest developments can be likened to evolutionary change in an animal population, with modifications occurring through changing frequencies in features already present in the population. Cultures may indeed change in this manner, but diffusion of ideas and techniques may also play an important role in culture change, as in the case of the introduction of Near Eastern musical instruments into Europe. The biological analogy here would be changes produced in a population by outbreeding. As we will demonstrate, most of the recent history of change in western music can be explained in terms of processes analogous to these. The analogies break down, however, in the most recent developments in western music, where there is a conscious and deliberate attempt by avant-garde composers to overthrow all tradition.

At first this attempt was phrased in terms of increasing freedom, by enlarging the timbral vocabulary. To this was added, however, the serial form of composition, which imposed a greater degree of syntactic rigidity than that found in the system it was supposed to replace. Randomness was seen as another way to free the composer from traditional forms. From randomness it was an easy step to proclaiming all sound potentially musical. It is in this context that the development of electronic devices for the production, modification, and recording of sound appeared. Electronic music represents the extrapolation of uniquely western technological and intellectual developments that are a radical departure from previous musical traditions.

The approach of a composer to electronic music is in many respects radically different from his approach to the composition of instrumental music. Although technology has simplified many of his tasks, it has placed greater responsibilities upon him. The composer knows that his work involves not only the conception but the realization of the composition as well. In this respect the various methods of composing electronic music vary only in the amount of time separating conception and realization. While this has varied from a few minutes (in the conventional tape studio) to several days (with the early computer pieces) it has become clear that in the next decade most composers will have instantaneous realization available to them in a semicomputerized studio. The composer might go about the process of composing in the following manner:

A small keyboard, similar to that of a typewriter, would be used to specify the original, electronically-generated material. Once specified, the sound would be played and the composer could make any changes desired. This material could then be stored in a computer memory and could be instantly recalled should the composer want to hear it again or develop the idea further. As new sections of the piece were composed they would be joined to the preceding material so that at any time the composer could review his work as it progressed. Once completed, the work would be transferred from the computer memory to recording tape and made available to the various "performance" media: radio, record companies, etc. The composer could carry out this process in his own home using a data-phone connection, and it would be possible for several composers to utilize the same facility simultaneously through some sort of time-sharing. If this proposal sounds far-fetched, the reader will be surprised to learn that this situation very nearly exists in the new electronic music studio of the Swedish Radio. Within ten years these procedures will be commonplace. It should be made clear that the computer is not composing the music but is merely generating, modifying, and storing musical materials at the direction of the composer.

The traditional method of composition—in which the composer notates his ideas, revises, recopies, copies parts, secures performers, rehearses, arranges performances, and finally records his music—now seems incredibly awkward. Even the traditional electronic music procedures—the recording, rerecording, and splicing of electronically-generated sounds on tape—seem cumbersome by comparison.

The amazing growth of electronic music in western culture during the last decade illustrates two points mentioned above: (1) transformation through modernization (in this case, technological advance) occurs easily and may even go unnoticed, and (2) the transformation may act as a stimulus for a fundamental reorganization of the great tradition.

The significance of electronic music, in which the composer deals directly with sound, lies not in the use of new material (concrète or electronically-generated sonorities) but in the fact that the composer is communicating directly with his audience without an intermediary. Whether or not this represents a return to an older tradition is less important than are the reasons for such an alteration at this point in our cultural development.

When Pierre Schaeffer first created aural collages of natural sounds at the Radiodiffusion Française in 1948, he was less concerned with the elimination of the performer than in creating a musical experience—one which, it so happened, could not be executed by instrumentalists.[7] The same can be said for the early tape-music created in 1952 by Vladimir Ussachevsky and Otto Luening at Columbia University.[8]

Nevertheless, their work made others who were familiar with electronic equipment realize the possibilities inherent in this new medium. So-called classical or serious music had, by 1950, become increasingly complex and difficult to perform. Composers had not ignored the pace of the technological age, and their music reflected the increased speed and variety of events that occur during any given period.

This music employs a tonal vocabulary which is more "efficient" than that of the music of the past, or its derivatives. This is not necessarily a virtue in itself, but it does make possible a greatly increased number of pitch simultaneities, successions, and relationships. This increase in efficiency necessarily reduces the "redundancy" of the language, and as a result the intelligible communication of the work demands increased accuracy from the transmitter (the performer) and activity from the receiver (the listener). Incidentally, it is this circumstance, among many others, that has created the need for purely electronic media of "performance."[9]

The growth of "efficiency" in the tonal vocabulary in electronic music, together with a constant decrease in redundancy, may be one of the primary barriers to the integration of electronic music into the cultural tradition out of which it is developing. Hockett[10] has compared traditional music with human spoken language. He has concluded that traditional music completely shares at least six of thirteen design features of language, partially shares two others, and that four features cannot be determined. Of these, *traditional transmission* is particularly important for our purposes, since all traditional music is passed on through learning, and the necessary learning takes place in the context of a cumulative cultural tradition. Given this fact, the resistance to composition in which randomness plays a part is quite understandable. This does not, however, explain the resistance to electronic music, since most of it is the very antithesis of the random. How are we to explain this fact? A clue may be found in another article of Hockett's in which, with regard to redundancy in the sound system of spoken language, he says:

> *In every human language, redundancy, measured in phonological terms, hovers near fifty percent.* The notion is that if redundancy tends to increase much above this figure, communication becomes inefficient and people speak faster or more sloppily. Decrease much below the figure leads to misunderstanding and people slow down or articulate more clearly. . . . It may be that this approximate figure is the rule for a wide variety of communicative systems, at least among human beings.[11]

If the same argument can be shown to hold for electronic music, we may have a key to the widespread (and largely unconscious) acceptance of some of it and the tenacious rejection of other aspects. It may be that these types of electronic music of most narrow acceptance are those in which redundancy is too low, making the work unintelligible, or too high, making it repetitious and boring. (See Morthenson, "Aesthetic Dilemmas in Electronic Music," below.—ED.)

Other reasons may cause this rejection aside from either a total break with traditional transmission or inadequate levels of redundancy. Rejection may reflect the failure of a new and complicated language to spread very rapidly. In this case, even though coded communications are being transmitted, the receivers of the messages are unable to decode them. Milton Babbitt was making this point when he said:

> The time has passed when the normal well-educated man without special preparation could understand the most advanced work in, for example, mathematics, philosophy, and physics. Advanced music, to the extent that it reflects the knowledge and originality of the informed composers, scarcely can be expected to appear more intelligible than these arts and sciences to the person whose musical education usually has been even less extensive than his background in other fields.[12]

We would be in error to ignore the increasing popularity of electronic music and its far-reaching commercial application. Techniques that originated in "advanced" composition are now being regularly applied to television and motion picture scores, popular teenage singing groups, singing commercials. At the present time, all that is unfamiliar about electronic music to the general public is its name.

It is worthy of note that the permeation of electronic music into the mass culture is controlled by middlemen (record, motion picture, and television producers) who are limited by the presumed sophistication of their audiences (ultimately a commercial consideration) to passing on what is deemed acceptable by an unsophisticated audience both qualitatively and quantitatively.

Thus the most significant area of change is in a new configuration of relationships between composition, performance, and listening. Surely here we find striking evidence of the characteristic interaction between great and little traditions, and of the fact that interaction between technology and the arts has begun.

To predict the course of a radical cultural change is in any circumstance a dubious enterprise. In the case we have been discussing it is doubly dangerous because, in contrast to other instances of great change, the attempted revolution in music has few precedents to which it can be compared. Despite this danger we feel that certain already apparent tendencies, if they continue, are at least suggestive of what may occur in the future. Of these, the roles of performer and composer seem the ones we can most likely predict.

At present most of those composers who are engaged in the composition of electronic music also compose music in the traditional manner. However, as we have pointed out above, the attempt to specify instructions for the performer in an ever more accurate manner has tended to make performers wary of attempting to perform modern music. If such a relationship between performer and composer persists, composers, now that other alternatives are for the first time open to them, may cease to compose in the traditional manner. Thus rather than being a participant in the dissemination of a developing tradition, the performer may become a specialist in the performance of a frozen corpus of composition. At the same time we may see once again the composer with direct control of communication with his audience, although not by combining his skills as composer with those of performer but instead, avoiding intermediaries between himself and his audience, directly controlling the electronic instruments producing the sounds to which his audience listens. The rapidity of creation and execution represented by modern electronic musical technology permits the composer to compose a piece of electronic music, have it released on a recording, and receive criticism in the mass media in the space of a few weeks. This is in marked contrast with the situation of the traditional composer, who had to find a performer or performers, wait for them to rehearse his piece, and only then obtain criticism. In the latter case the composer frequently was unsure of whether criticism was of his composition as originally conceived or of the performers' interpretation of it. This situation of ambiguity no longer holds under the conditions presented by the direct forms of communication and critical feedback that apply to electronic music. This is not to say that there will be no interaction between great and little musical traditions. Such interaction will, however, likely be between an electronic classical tradition and popular music rather than the traditional interaction of classical and folk music.

Conclusions

Our discussion has attempted to outline certain developments in recent musical history whose implications have been neglected, in the hope that we may stimulate others to carry on the preliminary analysis we have begun. We feel that the processes described here are as important as analogous changes in the arts in the past, such as the change from architectural to easel painting, to which art historians have devoted so much attention. It should be stressed that new concepts of time and space are equally influential in other aspects of the same technological revolution that we have described for music.[13] The contemporary technological revolution is not easily compartmentalized. Those who ignore its implications in areas outside of the political and economic may be missing an opportunity to study far-reaching cultural implications occurring at the same time.

Notes

1. Robert Redfield, "The Social Organization of Tradition," *The Far Eastern Quarterly* 15, no. 1 (1956).
2. William P. Malm. *Japanese Music and Musical Instruments* (Rutland, Vt., and Tokyo: Charles E. Tuttle Company, 1959), p. 265.
3. Revised and published as *The Musical Experience of Composer, Performer, Listener* (Princeton: Princeton University Press, 1950).
4. It should be noted that jazz is the product of an American little tradition originally drawing upon extrawestern elements, one in which improvisation is paramount.
5. Colin McPhee, *Music in Bali* (New Haven: Yale University Press, 1966), p. xvii.
6. Ibid., p. 8.
7. Pierre Schaeffer. *A la recherche d'une musique concrète* (Paris: Editions de Seuil, 1952).
8. Vladimir Ussachevsky, "As Europe Takes to Tape," *American Composers Alliance Bulletin* 3, no. 3 (Autumn 1953): 10.
9. Milton Babbitt, "Who Cares if You Listen?" *High Fidelity Magazine*, February 1958, p. 39.
10. Charles Hockett, "The Origin of Speech," *Scientific American*, September 1960.
11. Charles Hockett, "The Problem of Universals in Language," in *Universals of Language,* ed. Joseph Greenberg (Cambridge: MIT Press, 1963), chap. 1.
12. Babbitt, "Who Cares," 40.
13. At a recent meeting of the American Association for the Advancement of Science, K. Doxiades pointed out that any place on earth is accessible by jet travel from any other in twelve hours—this is approximately the same as the time it took the citizen of a city state to walk from its center to the border of it.

Electronic Music

Otto Luening
COLUMBIA UNIVERSITY

Before considering even the most elementary aesthetic values of
electronic music, one needs to review the uses and effects of
sound in the twentieth century. In this century man has demonstrated that sound can heal and sound can cause illness and death.
Ultrasonic vibrations are used in medical diagnosis, as a healing
force, and as a pain killer in dentistry. They are also used sometimes to mix chemicals and under some conditions as an insect
repellent. Infrasonic vibrations form an area of important research for defense departments, and their theoretical ramifications and practical applications belong to the destructive arts.

Urban sounds, factory sounds, and some music sounds, if un-
controlled, cause stress and hearing loss that can be severe. Not
only rock and roll music that is played too loud but the revered
classics and romantics can cause hearing damage if the loudspeaker becomes a *too-loud-speaker.*

To counterbalance this rather gloomy picture of the sound
world, music as therapy, as a healing art, is playing an increasingly
important part in modern life. But computers will continue to
enable us to extend the limits of sound production. How many of
the more complex findings that will be programmed and readily
be perceived by the human ear remains to be seen. Just how
sound vibrations perceived by other means (through headbones
or vibrations felt through the feet) affect us remains an un-
answered question. In this article sounds that produce physical
pain will be excluded from musical considerations.

Judging by the majority of electronic works known to this
author, differences between them and those using older means of
sound production also need to be briefly examined before even
elementary aesthetic considerations can be noted. Mere novelty

28

and shock have already become redundant and elementary aesthetic fodder of little value for a more sober aesthetic consideration of the new medium.

In electronic sound production, breathing pauses and the bowings that make phrasing possible in conventional music can be supplanted by the possibility of sustaining sounds indefinitely. At its best, it is alleged that this can produce a trancelike condition in the listener. At its worst, unless broken by pause and variety in dynamics, tempo and rhythm, trance becomes redundant and boring when too long, and static instead of hypnotic. If both too loud and too long, it can be physically damaging to the ear.

Electronic composers are capable of producing an endless variety of sound material. They have gotten some idea of balance and control from information theory. A somewhat oversimplified definition of this theory might be that unfamiliar material needs repetition and some redundancy to be perceived. More familiar material needs variation of one kind or another to keep it from becoming too redundant. Balancing these two approaches within a time span can create an organic balance (an acoustic balance) in an electronic world.

It has been fairly well established that the average listener in a concert hall finds it difficult to concentrate on electronic sound for a long time. This may be because staring at a loud speaker is not exactly a vivid aesthetic experience. Exceptions are found in those concert halls with multiple speakers, which enable the sound to be passed around various parts of the hall. Electronic sound outdoors or in large auditoriums does not raise these problems in the same way. Electronic sound in the theater, whether used in opera, stage plays, or ballet, has to be well controlled to keep from masking voices and words, and the visual aspects tend to temper the impression of coldness that much electronic sound evokes in the average listener. Multimedia events too can integrate electronic sound into a large time frame that can be quite convincing when viewed and listened to on its own terms.

When electrically produced sounds are combined with traditional instruments—whether a symphony orchestra, chamber music ensemble or a solo instrument—problems of mixing and masking arise. (See Morrill, "Loudspeakers and Performers," below. — Ed.) If electronic sounds are used with a symphonic ensemble as direct contrasts to the conventional instrumental sounds, the work can be much like the baroque concerto grosso. Either one of the sound groups can act as concertino or concerto. To use electronic sound as a section of a symphonic ensemble that blends with the other instruments necessitates careful calculation in the mixing of electronic sounds with those from conventional instruments, with particular attention paid to the problem of masking conventional sound by those that are electronically produced. This requires sophisticated electronic sound control but also a reevaluation of conventional orchestral practice. Many traditionally accepted and heretofore aesthetically satisfactory orchestral timbres do not mix well with those produced electronically.

This problem is even more in evidence in chamber and solo music that incorporates electronic sound. Once these balances have been mastered, the aesthetic considerations and responses are tied somewhat to those we are accustomed to in our responses to conventional, nonelectronic music. The process described is an evolutionary one, and electronic sound has become a new section of the orchestra, a new instrument of the ensemble, or a new accompanying instrument of the soloist. Works of this genre are an extension of previous aesthetic experiences, which include movies and television. There the electronic sound medium is subdued by the directors so that the visual and word images are not masked. It has in a way already been typed to fit supernatural and mystery pictures and sequences and sometimes to underline mental aberrations. If the picture is aesthetically rewarding, electronic sound plays an assigned part.

Under what conditions can purely electronic music best be perceived? For the specialist there is no problem; he listens attentively to the technical and expressive qualities of each piece like one virtuoso composer-pianist listening to another's work . . . a Rachmaninoff listening to Prokofiev. In the lighted stage of a concert hall, the visual bleakness of loudspeakers does not help the electronic sound to really communicate with the average or even trained listener. Perhaps art galleries, museums, planetariums, and libraries would be more suitable locations for electronic concerts.

With present day concert hall conditions, the best means for the electronic or computer composer to project his ideas to the average listener is to pay great attention to the organic form or gestalt of his piece. The basic sonority forms should be well defined. They could be called organic, which in this context means acoustic relationships. To achieve such clarity in this medium demands spacings, pauses, and rhythms in a time frame that best projects both the basic motive and the electronic sound itself.

While the mixed media use of electronic sound is evolutionary, the use of these sounds by themselves is revolutionary. Any attempt to sharply define expressivity and æsthetic values in this medium will probably evoke a sharp response from many quarters.

Ferruccio Busoni, in his *Sketch of a New Aesthetic of Music* (1907), wrote of Cahill's Dynamophone: "Only a long and careful series of experiments, and a continued training of the ear, can render this unfamiliar material approachable and plastic for the coming generation, and for Art."

Perhaps the avant-gardist of tomorrow may be tempted to investigate the area described in a book published by Orcus Research in Kansas City in 1971 called *Biomusic,* by Manfred Eaton. *Biomusic* described "a class of electronic systems that use biological potentials in feedback loops to induce powerful, predictable, repeatable psychological states which can be elegantly controlled in real time."

How our culture and present superculture and subculture will develop depends largely on whether social changes produce a world order with a world language and also how outer space explorations and developments will affect humanity. The electronic medium belongs to both spheres. In what way and to what extent our senses will adapt to the sound vibrations of today and tomorrow only time will reveal. Or is it possible that unless we are on guard, something akin to *Biomusic* will infringe, expand, or even take over what we today call music?

Electronic Music: Art beyond Technology

Daria Semegen
STATE UNIVERSITY OF NEW YORK, STONY BROOK

An electronic music sound recipe of today might go something like this: "To several dozen sine tones, add a cluster of high frequency-modulated square waves, throw in a dash of reverberation, a pinch of ring-modulation, strain through a voltage-controlled filter, switch on the sequencers and random voltage generators, stir all with a joystick" and . . . presto! . . . sit back and enjoy instant electronic music à la synthesizer, compliments of the wonders of voltage control. No more tape-splicing and best of all, no more nicked fingers; just throw away those old razor blades and splicing block: the voltage-controlled synthesizer has arrived, and electronic music has graduated from a blue- to a white-collar job.

Even some critical reviews of electronic music concerts and recordings have given the impression that any composer who bothers to place a tape onto a splicing block must surely be a nimble-fingered but otherwise mindless Neanderthal. He creates electronic music sounds that are somehow "old-fashioned" because they have simply been spliced together rather than emitted in streamlined automation by dozens of voltage-controlled devices.

Questions come to mind: Does such a composer err against technology, or does it really matter what specific technical means are taken to achieve a desired *musical* goal within the electronic music medium? Do all sound effects, yielded automatically by audio electronic devices with a minimum of the composer's authorship and involvement, instantly become *music* in the traditional sense of composition, or do they remain simply as sound effects without the benefit of the composer's cognizant and intuitive selection and shaping into a musical work? Is electronic music a product of technological conveniences destined to make the job of composing somehow "easier"? Is it a new musical philosophy? Is the medium of electronic gadgetry the only message electronic music needs to offer to listeners? Does electronic music suffer from artistic poverty? Is it destined to be the bane of all future music?

The generative question might be: Do we, or should we, listen, respond to, and evaluate electronic music as music per se or should such music be perceived only from the vantage point of a mystique of appreciation of advancement, complexity, and novelty of techniques and gadgetry used to produce the sounds? The latter would be a somewhat esoteric position available only to professionals in the audio field and a few knowledgeable composers, and all but inaccessible to the average music listener. *Caveat auditor!* (May the listener beware!). Surely, the listener should not be made to feel intimidated by technocratic attributes ascribed to electronic music works and should be free to listen to them as purely *music,* consisting of phrases, sound colors, progression of dramatic elements, and traits generally ascribed to instrumental music with which most listeners feel relatively familiar.

Some electronic music is created for or during "real-time" performance rather than for storage on tape for future listening in concert playback, for instance. Real-time performance on electronic instruments may be likened to live performance on traditional instruments in a loose sense. Although a certain amount of precomposition is possible with series of prearranged events (patches or settings of the controls) performed on/by the electronic instruments, real-time performance often involves composition in the form of improvisation to varying degrees. In this case, there is virtually no delay between the compositional idea, experiment, or even accident (chance) and its realization as live sound. The complexity and variety of sound patterns depends on the functional limitations of the electronic sound generation and modification equipment used. Real-time performance contrasts with writing a traditional score and waiting for a future performance to eventually realize it in sound. Although the traditional score seems tedious when compared with real-time composition/ performance, it may have the advantage of giving the composer time to reflect and form an objective view of the entire musical work, its structural components and overall shape, and to add or delete sounds in the process of evolving the essential details that form the unique basic language of the work. In the virtually instant results of real-time composition/performance, the additional time for reflection, which acts as a psychological buffer-zone for the composer's own creative feedback in evaluating sound choices, is less frequently available. Given the time limitations for creative reflection and setting of units' controls and the typical sound and gestural patterns characteristic of many synthesizer patches or settings, the resulting electronic music often may sound more like loosely related sound effects strung together and sharing the same time-space rather than an integral musical work that develops its own nuances of grammar and eventually speaks its own language to the listener. Inherent in this language is the particular manner and logic of selecting and combining elements characteristic of the composer's æsthetic sense for the purpose of expression and communication through musical sound composition.

Can involuntarily produced sound effects (electronic or other) always, ever, or never be considered music? It seems that music begins when sound effects stop—that is, stop being merely sound effects in their own right and are selected and designed into contexts that give them a meaningful function in the realization of the total language-expression within a musical work. In considering the realm of noncommercial electronic music that ventures to aspire beyond sound effects rather easily obtained by any electronic music aficionado, the composer presumably is concerned with creating an individual art work bearing the thumbprints of his or her creative personality while also representing those techniques leading toward its expression in the medium of electronic music. Any technological means that brings the composer closer to the desired musical goal is equally valid, without the need for apologies or the false suppostion that one means is somehow more superior *musically* than another. Ultimately, creative talent *combined* with craftsmanship is essential to the art of musical composition, since a musically promising work that contains technical flaws and various compositional deficits may have no advantage over a technically perfect but musically sterile one.

In the quest for individual expression in the electronic music medium, it is impossible to discount the reality of resultant sound textures and patterns recognized as typically characteristic of synthesizer design, which are intended to be readily duplicated by anyone familiar with any one system and its patching routines and are inevitably unoriginal. Likewise, it is impossible to discount the synthesizer's considerable utility and convenience when used to produce multilayered, intricate pitch patterns, each with its own rhythmic scheme, timbres, and amplitudes creating an elaborate soundscape whose realization on the synthesizer may take only several minutes of control setting compared with several hours or perhaps days of tape recording, overdubbing, and splicing to achieve a similar sound result in the basic classical tape studio. However convenient such automation may be for creating complex sound patterns, it can also result in monotextural, rhythmically monotonous, and seemingly endless and aimless perpetual motion, with randomly generated patterns eventually rambling on to a far distant *niente*.

Lacking the convenience of prepackaged synthesizer patching routines, a composer learning the art of electronic music composition in the down-to-basics environment of a conventional classical tape studio (without synthesizer) might be more economical, selective, and even by necessity more creative in choosing and dealing with sounds when faced with the time factor alone in conventional tape recording, sound manipulation, and editing techniques involved in producing original sound materials "from scratch." By retaining and exercising basic editorial control (including tape-splicing procedures) over the simpler and progressively more complex stages of a sound passage's development from the beginning of the studio work experience, the composer is able to gradually refine his skills of creative selection from the available sounds stored on tape. By taking time to evaluate and redesign juxtapositions of sounds on tape through comparative listenings and editing, it is possible to strike a balance between the rational and intuitive aspects of the compositional process. The experience of closely working with the generation and recombining of sounds on tape early in the composer's electronic music studio work is of essential value in any future dealings with sound materials generated by any technological means within the electronic music genre.

Synthesizer- or computer-generated sounds may be stored in a soundbank (tape or computer disc) for immediate or future use using the basic sound manipulation techniques learned in the classical studio. Individual sonorities or entire sound passages may be selected and spliced to form the final sound image, or splicing may simply be used for final touch-ups of an existing tape. Uniquely, tape splicing itself can generate new *hybrid sound sequences* (composed of juxtapositions of diverse sounds), which are not available by any other means. That is, the sounds in the passage would not ordinarily occur as the result of an automatic process of generation and actually would have to be spliced into a sequence in order to exist as a sequence.

When using magnetic tape as a primary sound storage medium, splicing is the constituent part of editing, giving the composer a tool similar to a painter's brush or a sculptor's chisel to add and delete sounds during the creation of an electronic music work, or any time afterward. So, dust off that splicing block, demagnetize the razor blade, play back the phrase that did not sound quite right, and experience the joy of splicing—or rather, its artistic rewards.

Murmur

Kenneth Gaburo

UNIVERSITY OF IOWA

MURMUR (herein defined as a quality) ONE: The apparent
    infinity
of sophisticated electronic music-making instruments designed
for and infinity of music(s) especially hoped for in the late
fifties and seen then by many as some kind of liberation from
the constraints of conventional electronic instruments
which in turn was some kind of liberation from conventional-
conventional instruments
e.g. orchestras
both states being liberations as well from musical sound-
    structures
and cultured positions closely associated with those conventional
instruments
has merely resulted in a new set of cultured positions
but significant constraints remain
for
if one accepts the proposition that the sound-generating-
    processing
system contains the composition within itself
then the constraint is a function of the instrument's potential
if
contrarily one accepts the proposition that the sound-generating
    processing
system is at best only the potential source for a composition
then the constraint is a function of the composer's head
but when the hoped-for infinity was promulgated it was so in the
absence of machines as we now know them excluding the RCA

Electronic Sound Synthesizer and embryogenic computer
    systems.

MURMUR TWO: The infinity, therefore, existed largely in the
    creative
imagination of the composer who once again believed himself
to have found a new region possibly sufficient, but clearly
    necessary,
to further express his intuitive and intellectual desires. What
he in fact found was a collection of (more properly an
    assemblage
of) electronic hardware, most of which were not designed for
compositional purposes (to say nothing of the infinity). That
environment is now generally referred to as the "classic"—
    frequently
expressed as a pejorative, in the light of the new instrumentation
—studio. To the extent that the term "classic" is used to force
some kind of distinction between the state of the art then and
what it has become, it is clearly inappropriate. Almost no studio
was of the first rank, or standard, or coherent as a system, or
fully-developed, or even yet of acknowledged excellence
    sufficient
to satisfy the composer well enough. Only potential existed.
    From
the technological point of view, that potential is now seen to have
been very low, while the current music-machine's potential is
    seen
to be very high. From the creative-qualitative point of view these
associations can easily be reversed because the search for the
instrument became as important as the search for the
    composition.
There was beauty in that search.

TRANSIENT ONE: The question of where the music was/is—in
the machine, in the head, or neither one exclusively—often had/
has to be temporarily arrested as one faced/faces the problems
of impedence mismatching, channel noise, audio fatigue,
    recalcitrant
engineers who refused/refuse to take us seriously, or electrical
shock due to improper grounding. The search, rather than
"classicism" or "dehumanization" was/is clearly there even in the
far more elegant RCA Columbia-Princeton Electronic Sound
Synthesizer, which, although designed for more trivial purposes,

quickly became/becomes an instrument when placed in the hands of
creative people. But not just search. For music came/comes.
To be sure, earlier works simply have to be regarded as back-breaking
fcats whcn mcasured against the machine's resistance
and the composer's own lack of technical knowledge. Even more
back-breaking now, because electronic composition is often confused
with technology or temporarily aborted because of the emphasis
on learning what the latest gadget does that the previous
one did not do, resulting directly from earlier primitive first-
associations with the machine-instrument, which was expected to
respond in more than a utilitarian manner and which caused
immediate outcries for more efficient instruments, thereby installing
for the first time to my knowledge the collusion/collision between
efficiency and the creative act. The devaluation of the splice was
inevitably a high-priority item in any cultivated discussion although
in my opinion it became/becomes one of the supreme moments
of decision-making in the compositional process second only to
the eraser and deserves special mention as a measure of the importance
of second thoughts/thoughts.

ELABORATION OF MURMUR TWO: There is a strange parallel between
the glorious junkshop referred to as the "classic" studio
and the current rage for personal, home-made instruments, bypassing
rather significantly the wide range of sophisticated instruments
now available.

Bypass, because as electronic instrumentation becomes more refined
technically and its generation-processing components become
more precise, the machine becomes, paradoxically enough,
more, not less, closed as a viable system. It is true that this
criticism was leveled against the assemblage studio as well. Now,
however, one clearly runs the risk that the inherent technical
perfection of the machine (a distinct advantage) designed to serve

precise musical functions will cause it to maintain its own sound-
identity no matter what (a distinct disadvantage). In the earlier
circumstance the sound-identity of a given instrument, say an
audio oscillator, was too uninteresting in itself to be maintained
compositionally (a distinct advantage) and the if-at-all-available
processing devices were frequently unpredictable (a distinct
disadvantage).

Bypass, because with more refined equipment composers
    become
readily caught up in the fascinating *means* by which sound-
    complexes,
emanating *directly* from the instrument, may be produced.
To some, the process becomes as important as the result. To
others, this condition is quite unacceptable. At the same time,
the "natural" beauty of these sound-complexes is often so
    compelling
that the composer's intellectual capacity is frequently obfuscated
by the machine's sensual capacity. To some composers this is a
value. To others, first sounds, no matter how elegant,
are to be distrusted. Furthermore, these sound-complexes, which
are a function of an instrument's peculiar qualities, generally
    hold
for *n* instruments of a kind. This characteristic militates rather
strongly against individual uniqueness when such uniform
instrumentation is utilized by *m* composers. To some, this form
    of
"group" association is consoling. To others, the only reasonable
answer is to move elsewhere. Therefore, the parallel to earlier
activity with respect to the current bypass condition is again, the
search. The difference lies partially in the fact that earlier
many composers *faced* black boxes, while now many try to *make*
    them.
Crucially, the search for the instrument on the way to the
composition has become the search for the composition on the
    way
to the instrument. And, one learns quickly that not all
    unijunction
transitors classified technically as substitute-equivalents
produce, qualitatively, the same sound at all.
    Bypass, because the efficiency and directness of the new
instrumentation has caused it to be quickly absorbed by
    commercial

culture or relegated to the position of being used as teaching
instruments; or because its sophistication comes too late for some
who have moved elsewhere; or because of computers; or because
the
desire to probe *into* the machine itself, instead of *in front* of it,
is so compelling; or because electronic music and its concepts
have
in turn influenced the way we think about conventional nonelectronic
instruments, resulting in a return to them in fascinating new
ways.
But return is not altogether proper here. For, since the late
fifties, some of us have been interested in the structured
synchrony-potential of music-machines, concrète sources, and
live
performers. The intrinsic beauty of concrète sources and live
performers (in my case weighted in favor of the voice, each
sample
of which carries its own special nuance), seemed less a reaction
to the machine in order to keep the music "human" than it was
to
raise the properties of the machine (never sufficient) to a
level of respectability. These components are still necessary in
my opinion, only now so in order to *reduce* the level of the
sophisticated machine to the point where it is not omnipresent.

EXPLICATION OF MURMUR ONE:
    Will I recognize the sound I want when I have heard it?
    Will I want the sound I have heard when I recognize it?
    Will I recognize the sound I have heard when I want it?
    Will I have heard the sound I want when I recognize it?
    Will I want the sound I recognize when I have heard it?
    Will I have heard the sound I recognize when I want it?

This set of charges to myself has served me well. Moreover,
if one substitutes, say,
"the structure," or
"the identity," e.g., my compositional identity, or
"the music-machine," for
"the sound" in the above set,
the logic of the set is unchanged,
although the *sense* in which the so-charged set of charges exists
is clearly transformed in each case.

A PARTIAL DISSOLUTION OF THE TRANSIENT: In the
  interim I have
developed a gentle respect for the machine, although I do not
  know
any more than I did about whether it is I who have a resistance
  to
it or the other way around. (Is it a peace treaty we have?)
Without wishing to establish an equivalence statement, I believe
  it
to possess human-like qualities. It is not infallible, nor is it
infinite in its musical attributes. It is as temperamental as I and
frequently much clearer. (You either conduct or you don't). A
  given
module, morever, is unquestionably idiosyncratic. The trick is to
treat the music-machine *as if* it were human in order to maintain
  its
uniqueness. (It is interesting to note that among other criteria,
your component specifications are frequently given in terms of
  their
life span). By getting into its guts, either through changing
components via home-made circuit fabrication or deeply
  investigating
the properties of a commercial product, the music-machine
  becomes
variable, possibly even flexible. And if not infinite, then
abundantly resourceful. (I'll try not to kick you anymore.) There
develops in the compositional process a sensual *and* intellectual
interplay between us, and ultimately we come to some
  agreement,
the machine and I, for the completed work has neither been as
  much
as I wanted nor as little as I could find acceptable. (Feedback
works!) Still, we lack technology in the area of controls,
especially in real-time performance. The current thinking by
some engineers is that we may have to give up that fantasy.
Question: When will it be possible for one individual to manage
  all of the controls necessary in order to produce a structured,
real-time composition? (Perhaps we should enter into a
  conspiracy?)

Some Practical Aesthetic Problems of Electronic Music Composition

David Keane
QUEEN'S UNIVERSITY

It has been observed from time to time in the recent past that little attention has been focused on the practical aesthetic problems of electronic music composition, while an impressive amount of print and verbage have been devoted to technical areas that presumably only support the higher level concerns of compositional aesthetics.[1] While I can do very little to equalize this considerable imbalance, I feel compelled to try to make some observations, or at least, formulate some questions that may be useful to us as listeners and particularly as composers and teachers. I would like to make clear from the outset that what I am presenting here is not a manifesto for a particular aesthetic view of electronic music composition; it is merely an early attempt to understand what seem to be highly intuitive processes on the part of the listener and particularly on the part of the composer.

A major obstacle to approaching problems related to the compositional process is the difficulty observing others or even oneself while engaged in creative processes. Self-consciousness intrudes upon an observed individual and considerably inhibits the creative process itself. Rudolf Arnheim reports that:

> Paul Valery, addressing a congress of surgeons in 1944, went so far as to suggest that the vital importance of a mental function can be measured by the degree to which that function is intolerant of attentive consciousness. In other words, there are functions that prefer the shadow to the light, or at least the twilight—that is, that minimum of

conscious awareness which is necessary and sufficient to make these acts to come about or to bait them. If failure or blocking is to be avoided, the cycle of sensation and motor activity must take its course without observations or interruptions, from its origin to the physiological limit of the performed act. This jealousy, this kind of modesty of our automatisms, is quite remarkable. One could derive a complete philosophy from it, which I would summarize by saying: Sometimes I think and sometimes I am.[2]

An initial and considerable difficulty in exploring the problems of the compositional process is the lack of a direct way of examining it. Given that restriction, there are some aspects that have an impact upon the compositional process that can be examined to some degree, and I would like to look at those.

The electronic music studio imposes a rather unique and important limitation upon the composer. For the most part he is unable to pursue his art anywhere but in the studio. While he can engage in considerations of processes, techniques, and structures anywhere, the actual assembly must take place almost entirely within the confines of the studio. The complexity and specificity of the studio situation can impose a considerable influence on a composition, to the point of modifying or even totally revising the composer's original intuitions and conceptions of an electronic sort. Primarily, this influence—both in the form of the limitations of generation of modification imposed by the equipment and of biases owing to the actual generation of sound during the interim states of assembly of the composition—is exerted as the composer works in the studio. The difference between a choreographer or a sculptor (artists who also realize their creations in a studio) and a composer of electronic music is that access is often very much more restricted for the composer. He can work only when no one else is working, he is dependent on an expensive facility that he must share with others, and the sophisticated contents of the studio need maintenance and modification, not infrequently at times the composer would like to use the studio.

The composer has not only to deal with having to adapt himself to work when the studio is available rather than when he is motivated to work but also with irregular patterns. In his essay on the dialectical phenomenology of creativity, Albert Hofstadter remarks:

There is but one way to practice creativity, namely to practice it. Practice means: imagine what to do and try to do it; then observe what you have done, comparing it with what you had imagined, and consider what has next to be done—whether the image has to be changed, or the doing, or both; to reimagine what has to be done and then do it; and so on. And practicing means: doing it steadily, every day. When you practice drawing, or the violin, or skating, you do it for several hours a day. [To practice creativity] . . . the task is to practice it attentively and thoroughly, just as you would if you wanted to play the violin or skate on ice.[3]

But creativeness in electronic music creation cannot very well be practiced, as I have pointed out, anywhere but in the electronic music studio. The electronic music composer, then, must be able to channel his creative energies into particular time periods. It is my belief that this time consideration has a considerable effect on the content of electronic music compositions. These time constraints are of three varieties: (1) optimum time periods, conducive to the composer's creativity, are often not available owing to institutional (rather than domestic) locations of the workspace; (2) inability to work in extended time periods and/or in a regular work pattern, conditions usually necessary for efficient, concentrated work; (3) the desire to modify or supplement the physical plant in which the work is carried on, producing impediments to the concentrated flow of musical ideas and creating additional time constraints.

Whether or not any of these restrictions can be eliminated, for the present they exert an influence on the musical output of electronic music composers. I will suggest how this influence interacts with the very essence of the musical work.

When a potential composer of electronic music confronts his medium, it is immediately apparent that the initial obstacle is the infinite number of possibilities. When a composer chooses to write for solo voice or orchestra, his medium places a multitude of restrictions upon him. The ranges, timbre possibilities, loudness possibilities force him to constantly adjust, modify, and revise his intentions in order to convey the essence of his musical idea in a real-time situation. On the other hand, because any sound, acoustically-generated or otherwise, is a potential sound source; because any acoustical sound source that is not accessible to the composer can be simulated, at least to a certain degree; and because studio work allows non-real-time performance; the composer is theoretically restricted only by his imagination and his competence for operating his equipment. With such vast potential, electronic music-making requires the composer to make a great many more essentially arbitrary decisions about the boundaries of the material he will employ in a composition. Too often, the electronic music composer is unable to adequately limit his sound resources to the point that it is possible to give the kind of cohesiveness to his composition that a successful piece of music requires. Too often the result is more a catalog of related possibilities of his system rather than a work that develops and explores fully the potentials of a few fertile musical ideas.

Leonard B. Meyer observes that

> evidently the operation of some principle of psychic economy makes us compare the ratio of musical means invested to the informational income produced by this investment. Those works are judged good which yield a high return. Those works yielding a low return are found to be pretentious and bombastic.[4]

Gestalt psychology generally defines "goodness" as regularity, symmetricality, simplicity—those tendencies that lead to comfortable levels of predictability. The fundamental axiom of Gestalt theory is the law of Prägnanz, which states that psychological organization will always be as "good" as prevailing conditions will allow.[5]

We resolve information, including sets of musical objects, into the simplest possible set. That is, when we encounter collections of related entities we tend to assume that they are drawn from a repertoire no larger than one that would account for the entities that we have observed. We do not normally attempt to consider possibilities of entities that might also be in that collection or repertoire but are not in evidence or in some way implied. The composer must then consider the repertoire implications of the sonic qualities of his material, not merely the procedural ones. Certainly, this is a particularly important point for novice composers. A repertoire implication that is too large, intentionally or otherwise, provides the listener with too many possibilities to make predictions or to observe interrelationships—the result is apparent randomness. I will come back to randomness shortly.

The numbers of knobs in the electronic music studio are perhaps an even greater obstacle to the composer than the numbers of sonic possibilities. Electronic compositions very frequently evolve using a logic of knobs and switches—proceeding in directions that are suggested by the physical ease of the control of sound manipulation rather than in directions suggested by the sound itself. For example, rapid glissandi over a wide range are frequent in electronic music compositions simply because they can be easily produced by a simple turn of a control. Such sounds are often obtrusive or even actually unpleasant. Electronic music is often too loud, too violent, simply because such loudness and violence can be so effortlessly produced. In fact, I wonder if the electronic music composer does not have a unique situation in that he deals with primarily *abstract* sonic material—abstract in the sense that most of his sounds are neither produced by or even simulate sounds that might be produced by physical force emanating from the body. In instrumental or vocal music as well as any other artistic endeavor that comes immediately to mind, the gestures assembled by the artist are either the direct result of proportional force and/or restraint, or, as in the case of the composer, the poet, or the choreographer, the gesture must be experienced vicariously as the ideas for a work are assembled. Electronic music generation makes possible sonic gestures that are not proportional to the physical bodily force exerted to produce the gesture. Moreover, sounds and sequences can be produced in the electronic music studio whose magnitudes of force are not necessarily entirely anticipated by the composer. Certainly, once the sounds are made, if not before, the composer exercises his judgment as to the appropriateness of the sonic gestures to the composition. I simply ask, does the lack of a direct relationship between the composer's own energies, or vicariously experienced energies, and the energy of the musical result exert an influence on the effectiveness of a work in the electronic medium?

Perhaps the most unique aspect of electronic music is the composer's ability to control each parameter of the music essentially independent of the other parameters—or at least we have that illusion. To quote Meyer:

> . . . the parameters of music do not as a rule move congruently. If they did, a passage would either be entirely on-going and without distinguishable internal organization, or it would be decisively closed— without connection with what follows. Because the parameters do not move congruently, there are degrees of closure; and these are at times quite subtle. The degree of closure, or alternatively of mobility, depends upon the shaping of the particular parameters at work, the degree of articulation contributed by each, and the number of parameters promoting or preventing closure.[7]

The ease of wide-ranging control of any particular parameter allows the composer to overfocus on a single parameter to the neglect of others. What may be forgotten is that single parameter control is really only theoretical—that each parameter exerts an influence on the perception of the others. Juan Roederer points out,

> First, the pitch sensation caused by a pure tone of fixed frequency may change slightly if we change the intensity: conversely the loudness of a tone of constant intensity will appear to vary if we change the frequency. Second, the sensation of loudness of a superposition of several tones of different pitch each is not anymore related in a simple way to the total sound energy flow; for a succession of tones of very short duration on the other hand, it depends on how long each tone actually lasts. Third, refined timbre perception . . . is a process that utilizes much more information than just the spectrum of a tone, the transient attack and decay characteristics are equally important.[8]

Murray Schafer states:

> . . . the three chosen parameters [intensity, frequency, duration] should never be regarded as insoluble or independent functions. At least as far as our perception of them is concerned, they are in constant interaction. For instance, intensity can influence time perceptions (a loud note will sound longer than a soft one), frequency will affect intensity perceptions (a high note will sound louder than a low one of the same strength) and time will affect intensity (a note of the same strength will appear to grow weaker over time)—to give just a few examples of interaction. In introducing students to the properties of sound I have noticed frequent confusion between notions as elementary as frequency and intensity and have come to the conclusion that the standard acoustic diagram is not only ambiguous but for some people, at least, may not correspond at all with the natural instincts of aural perception. The problems between acoustics and psychoacoustics may never be clarified as long as the 3-D acoustic image continues to be regarded as an inviolably accurate model of a sound event.[9]

The electronic medium allows the musical parameters to be pushed to the limits of perception. At these frontiers the composer faces some special problems beyond simply influencing the perception of associated parameters. The rate and degree of change of sound events can be so extreme that they nullify the effect and perception of controlled change, even to the extent that the perception of the changes themselves are nullified. Where the change is fast, constant, and extreme the listener experiences a dulling sense of uneventfulness, the ironic consequence of such extreme information rates.[10] Yet it is so easy with programming devices like sample-and-hold circuits and sequences or with tape speed variation capabilities to operate on the frontiers of duration perception. The composer, tainted with knowledge of the underlying detail, may not himself experience the dulling effect, and as surrogate receiver he must be wary of such pitfalls. Frequently, electronic music composers are guilty of monotony in their compositions, owing, I suspect, in a large measure to this very circumstance.

The lower threshold of intensity, like the upper and lower thresholds of frequency and duration, is simply a region in which perception of that particular mode ceases. The upper threshold of intensity is not characterized by such gentle dissipation, defined as "the threshold of pain." Leo Küpper points out that "strong dynamics, linked to an urgent, even an aggressive, need for expression is one of the more common faults of electro-acoustic music."[11] Certainly it is such high dynamic levels, or the threat of them, that keeps a substantial proportion of potential audiences for electroacoustic music away from concerts.

Another threshold that must be mastered by the composer of electronic music is the interval. I am referring not only to the melodic interval of frequency but the linear distances in any parameter. We can perceive extremely small differences in frequency and energy when the sounds are isolated. But when sound is heard in the context of other sounds, our perception varies greatly with the nature of the fabric of the total sound event—the more dense the vertical band, the larger the melodic intervals that can be distinguished. Moreover, the noisier the context, the larger the melodic and dynamic intervals must be.[12]

Random intervals, or apparently random intervals, are frequently a major component of new music, and random structural components are produced with great facility in the electronic medium. While randomness contributes to stylistic identification, there is some question as to how significantly it can play a role in a work that may be considered successful. Wallace Berry states:

. . . *controlled contextual function* of element-events is of fundamental value and, even, of necessity in musical communication where the respondent is engaged in apprehensions of *functional ordered relations* as aspects of experience. The view that purely superficial sound qualities in individual isolation—*or in adventitious association*—have a primitive communicative potential suggests some kind of noncontextual significance, even though an important aspect of any "meaning" in the isolated event (say, a big tutti attack in the orchestra) is normally the *expectation it arouses* with respect to likely subsequent events. At the same time, however, the most important aspect of musical experience derives from the *interactions and interrelations* of contiguous and con-current events of differing qualities *within contextual procedures deter-mined by controlled lines* of progressive and recessive successions. Such a concept of meaning is not applicable where event-confluences are random and arbitrary.[13]

Andre Moles presses further to say:

One of the fundamental characteristics of the human receptor is the existence of a maximum *limit* to the flow of perceptible information. When this maximum flow is exceeded, the individual selects, with the aid of criteria derived from his previous experience, forms from the message presented to him. Forms are abstractions, elementary stages of intelligibility. If these criteria fail him, the individual is over-whelmed, left behind by the originality of the message; he loses interest.

The message most difficult to transmit is that without redundancy (with maximum information), hence without any a priori *form*. It is both easiest to give an approximate picture of it and most difficult to give an exact picture of it. It is the most fragile of messages. Inter-estingly, this message is most devoid of esthetic value—and of a priori meaning.[14]

The composer of electronic music must maintain vigilance over the degree to which randomness structures his work if the work is to be meaningful to the listener. Random structures bring up the whole question of the role of prefabricated structures—those assemblies that are in some degree determined by an electrical rather than a mental process. How much does the arrangement of material depend on the man-machine interface itself? Stephen Smoliar has written that

. . . it is very difficult to specify the nature of . . . a high level language [which can operate at the sonological level]. In fact, it is unclear that such a language exists. Electronic music is still very much a matter of ad hoc experimentation and editing, and Music V may have proven even detrimental to the evolution of a theory of electronic music in that many composers have substituted the goal of achieving an elegant program for that of creating a piece of music which satisfies their personal tastes [see Melby "*Computer* Music or Computer *Music*," be-low.—ED.] This is the very act of dehumanization which people tend to fear in the computer revolution; and, in this case, the damage may, unfortunately, be irrecoverable.[15]

I am not prepared to go so far as to say that the direction of electroacoustic music has in some way been irretrievably damaged. After all, it is only the medium that is affected by trends in the medium, whatever the trends are. Human ears and human minds continue to function in much the same way they always have. But approaches that satisfy the needs of machines rather than the needs of musical listeners (including, or perhaps, especially, composers) are not entirely fruitful ones.

What concerns me more is what obstacles, if any, the hands-on process of electronic music has on the creative process. Does the process of generating random, in-part-random or otherwise in-part-determined-by-the-machine material interfere in a significant way with the normal functioning of the mind in a creative task situation?

On the other hand, do simple one-to-one relationships in sound generation with control devices, particularly computer graphics systems, allow *too* precise a conceptualization or visualization (if I may use the term in the context of the imagination of sonic events)? How much does the ability to toy with a sonic idea acoustically intrude upon the ability of the composer to toy with the idea mentally? With only intuition to support the notion, I am inclined to believe that the real does invade the composer's capacity to conceptualize the ideal.

Anton Ehrenzweig deals with the problems of precise visualization:

It is not an advantage if the creative thinker has to handle elements that are precise in themselves such as geometric or architectural diagrams. Their near perfect gestalt appeals too much to that gestalt principle and its law of closure. They resist the [dynamic process by which the ego scatters and represses surface imagery] needed for fruitful unconscious scanning. Hadamard came to the conclusion that the use of diagrams in doing geometry—I am thinking of course of creative inventions—is misleading because their neatness is apt to obscure the complexity of a problem. He trained himself to ignore the good gestalt of such diagrams and purposely diverted his attention to some, in itself meaningless, detail. The subjective destruction of the good gestalt is needed even if the material which is to be handled objectively possesses qualities of good gestalt. . . .

Hadamard suggests that Greek geometry lost its creative impetus in Hellenistic times because of too precise visualization. It produced generations of clever computers and geometers, but no true geometricians. Development in geometric theory stopped altogether. Descartes broke the deadlock by doing away with precise visualization and the seduction of neat diagrams. He invented analytical geometry which expressed geometric relationships by visualization of a stable space grid. We are faced with dynamic interaction between several shifting space systems. No precise focusing is possible. No wonder that space intuition is the rarest of gifts among mathematicians. . . .

. . . academic teaching is wont to put a premium on powers of precise visualization, not only in the arts, but also in music or in science, and certainly also in logic. I would explain this insistent demand for precision in academic teaching as a defensive secondary process in a psychoanalytic sense; the slighted surface faculties try to suppress unconscious scanning in order to retain full control of the working process. The necessary blurring of conscious focusing is felt as a danger and a threat of total chaos. This fear may be only another aspect of the more general misunderstanding of unconscious participation in creative work. Hadamard's recommended procedure in the use of diagrams in geometry displaces the emphasis from important gestures to insignificant details. How easily could this advice be constructed as encouragement of chaos! The displacement of proper emphasis is a typical primary-process technique. It is not easy for dry academicians to accept that syncretistic primary-process techniques rather than analytic clarity of detail are needed by the creative thinker to control the vast complexities of his work.[16]

Ehrenzweig maintains that truly creative decisions are made by allowing the subconscious to scan virtually all of the possible choices and, after making a selection in this informed way, allowing the result to be passed on to the conscious. The subconscious scanning is carried on in momentary lapses of concentration or when the conscious mind is engaged in completely unrelated tasks. However, for this process to function it is necessary for the individual to *know* the possibilities or the means for arriving at the possible choices, in order to have a clear comprehension of the set from which the choice is to be made. When an event or sequence is extracted from electrical components that generate random material or, conversely, allow too narrow a range within the set, subconscious scanning may be short-circuited. Is this the case? If so, what can be done to free the composer from the restriction?

We must make a distinction between complexity that is arbitrary and contrived and complexity that is rich in relationships within the composition. Complexity can be examined on two levels. One is a structural description—the music is *constructed* of X elements of Y types. The other is a functional description—*action* takes place in X direction at a Y rate.[17] Electronic music composers have for a good number of years focused too much on structure and too little on function in the sense of progression or movement.

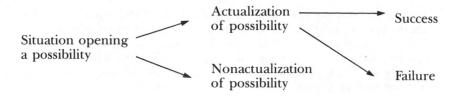

At every stage there is a choice. Bremond compares the structure of any narrative to the flight of an arrow:[18]

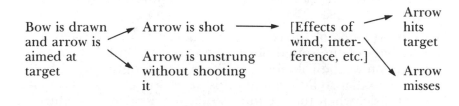

In literature, Andre Jolles identified nine simple forms in literature—forms that were simply unfilled possibilities. Etienne Souriau broke the forms down into six basic kinds of force and five methods of combination of the forces. Vladimir Propp identified thirty-one events in fixed order—he found that however many of the thirty-one events a tale had, they always appeared in the same order. Claude Bremond, however, asserts that the basic narrative unit is not the event but the sequence and that a literary work, no matter how long or complex, is comprised of an interweaving of sequences. He represents the basic scheme as:

In music, too, it is not so much the sonic event itself that is significant as the meaning of the event in a progression towards another point. It is the trip itself, not so much as the signposts along the way, that makes the experience of a piece of music rewarding. In distinguishing between phonetics and phonology, Saussure said:

> Just what phonational movements could accomplish if language did not exist is not clear; but they do not constitute language. [Language] is a system based on the neutral opposition of auditory impressions, just as a tapestry is a work of art produced by the visual oppositions of threads of different colours. The important thing in analysis is the role of oppositions, not the processes through which the colours were obtained.[19]

In a description of his work on *Hymnen,* Karlheinz Stockhausen takes the importance of function in a composition a step further.

What I use is the mutation process of nature, that's what music is all about. It's an intermodulation so that one being can become another. I'm not interested in collage. I'm interested in revealing how, at a special moment, a human sound is that of a duck and a duck's sound is the silver sound of shaking metal fragments. All these sounds are interrelated very subtly. Just by the manner in which you listen to them and in the way they're exposed in time and fairy tales are about this: the straw that the miller's daughter has to weave into gold in Rumpelstiltskin, for example . . . Transubstantiation—like the mystical moments in religion when the water is transformed into wine.[20]

Because so much of the composer's energy is concentrated upon the creation of the sound object, he may have little left over for the creation of the role for that object in a progression. I find it remarkable that so little attention is given to progression in electronic music, when the medium so facilitates such procedures. I find it even more remarkable that attention to progression seems to come more from the composers using concrète sources rather than those who use synthesizers, when the less plastic nature of concrète material is much less yielding to assembly into progressions. Perhaps the phenomenon is related to the points I have raised concerning richness of resources and the potential for successful subconscious scanning. Given a limited number of concrète sources, the set of possibilities becomes very finite indeed.

Victor Shklovsky suggests that process in art is important at a level beyond the one we have already examined:

Art exists to help us recover the sensation of life; it exists to make us feel things, to make the stone stony. The end of art is to give a sensation of the object as seen, not as recognized. The technique of art is to make things "unfamiliar," to make forms obscure, so as to increase the difficulty and the duration of perception. The act of perception in art is an end in itself and must be prolonged. In art, it is our experience of the process of construction that counts, not the finished product.[21]

However wary the composer is, whatever his objectives are, it is the nature of art that the composer can never rest easy that he has mastered his medium. As soon as he has discovered how to achieve an artistic end, he must begin to look for another artistic end to achieve. Unlike the cabinet-maker, the composer cannot repeatedly produce the same work. Jos Kunst described the phenomenon this way:

Poetical semantics seem to be bound up with a certain bending-of-the-rules of natural language semantics. What is at issue here must, I think, be characterized as an *unlearning-plus-learning* process: (at least) a habit is broken (unlearning), and new intelligence is gained concerning it and the conditions it is related to (learning). These unlearning-plus-learning processes, if indeed they are essential to poetical semantics, go far in explaining why there seems to be no precise *point of closure* of the poetical competence.[22]

It is perhaps due to both the beauty and the curse of art that we seem to endlessly seek answers to questions like the ones set forth in this paper. Even when we feel we have found some answers to the questions, if we ever do, it only invites a larger and more perplexing set of questions. The occasional posing of the right question, however, may allow us glimpses of immeasurable value even if we cannot arrive at an entirely satisfactory answer. We shall never understand the workings of art and the human mind if we do not *attempt* to understand, no matter how poor our tools are for the job.

Notes

1. Lucien Goethals, "Considerations," *Faire* 4/5 (1978): 22–23. Jose Marie Neves, "Education by and for Electroacoustic Music: Topics for Reflection," *Faire*, 4/5 (1978): 37. David Keane, "The Fine Arts: The Nature, Role and Future," in *An Image of the Whole: Knowledge and Curriculum in an Age of Fragmentation*, ed. William Higgenson (Kingston: Canadian Centre for Integrative Education, 1977), p. 28.

2. Rudolf Arnheim, "Notes on Creativity," in *Essays on Creativity*, ed. Stanley Rosner and Lawrence E. Abt (Croton-on-Hudson, N.Y.: North River Press, 1974), p. 8.

3. Albert Hofstadter, "On the Dialectical Phenomenology of Creativity," in *Essays in Creativity*, ed. Stanley Rosner and Lawrence E. Abt (Croton-on-Hudson, N.Y.: North River Press, 1974), p. 146.

4. Leonard B. Meyer, *Music, the Arts and Ideas* (Chicago: University of Chicago Press, 1967), p. 37.

5. K. Koffka, *Principles of Gestalt Psychology* (New York: Harper and Bros., 1945), p. 110.

6. David Keane, "The Fine Arts: The Nature, Role and Future," in *An Image of the Whole: Knowledge and Curriculum in an Age of Fragmentation*, ed. William Higgenson (Kingston: Canadian Centre for Integrative Education, 1977), p. 28.

7. Leonard B. Meyer, *Explaining Music* (Berkeley: University of California Press, 1973), p. 88.

8. Juan G. Roederer, *Introduction to the Physics and Psychophysics of Music* (New York: Springer Verlag, 1975), p. 4.

9. R. Murray Schafer, *The Tuning of the World* (Toronto: McClelland and Steward, 1977), pp. 125–26.

10. Wallace Berry, *Structural Functions in Music* (Englewood Cliffs, N.J.: Prentice-Hall, 1976), p. 17.

11. Leo Küpper, "New Possibilities of Vocal Music," *Faire* 4/5 (1978): 31–36.

12. Jonathan Cott, *Stockhausen: Conversation with the Composer* (New York: Simon and Schuster, 1973), p. 95.

13. Berry, *Structural Functions in Music*, p. 17.

14. Andre Moles, *Information Theory and Esthetic Perception*, trans. Joel E. Cohen (Urbana: University of Illinois Press, 1966), p. 74.

15. Stephen W. Smoliar, "Music Programs: An Approach to Music Theory through Computational Linguistics," *Journal of Music Theory* 20, no. 1 (1976): 120.

16. Anton Ehrenzweig, *The Hidden Order of Art* (St. Albans: Paladin, 1970), p. 57–58.

17. Andre Moles, *Information Theory*, p. 35.

18. Robert Scholes, *Structuralism in Literature: An Introduction* (New Haven: Yale University Press, 1974), p. 96.

19. Ferdinand de Saussure, *Course in General Linguistics*, trans. Wade Baskin (London: Peter Owen, 1964), p. 33.

20. Cott, *Stockhausen*, p. 151.

21. Scholes, *Structuralism*, pp. 83–84.

22. Jos. Kunst, "Making Sense in Music: The Use of Mathematical Logic," *Interface* 5, nos. 1–2 (1976): 5.

Aesthetic Dilemmas in Electronic Music

Jan W. Morthenson
STIFTELSEN EMS STOCKHOLM, SWEDEN

I have chosen to discuss "dilemmas" instead of "problems" in electronic music. The distinction is, of course, in many instances rather subtle. "Dilemma" means a choice between alternatives equally undesirable. In logic, it means an argument that presents an antagonist with alternatives equally conclusive against him, whichever he chooses. So, to be confronted with a dilemma is not exactly the same as to be confronted with a problem. A problem may have a more or less satisfactory solution; a dilemma, however, cannot be resolved by following simple logical steps, such as in mathematics. The dilemma-decision is subjective; you risk something personally. It's the constant companion of the creative artist. For a while you are permitted to be experimental, but sooner or later you have to face the crucial realities of aesthetic dilemmas again. To experiment in an aesthetic sense does not mean that you find a general solution to a problem. Artistic aspects are dynamic, even dialectic.

If we disregard more extreme cases of decision-making in musical composition—such as total serialism, I-Ching chance operations, control by mathematical formulas, and the like—aesthetic dilemmas for the composer go with almost any note or sound in both instrumental and electronic music. It may be argued, however, that some dilemmas are more typical for electronic music.

For theoretical reasons, electronic music should in this context be understood in a more classic sense. Live electronic music and far-reaching aleatoric or random procedures represent special categories. Also, mixed-media pieces, in which electronic music is only a part, have their own dilemmas and problems. Traditional

---

From *Dansk Musiktidskrift,* no. 2 (1981/1982): 47–61.

and strict electronic or computer music, composed and put together in a rather conventional manner, raise enough questions. Also, the advantage of classic examples is that one can make extrapolations to more unusual applications, whereas the reverse is difficult.

Now, how do "aesthetic" dilemmas differ from technical or other dilemmas in the making of electronic music? It is well known that the term "aesthetic" is interpreted in many ways, not only amateurishly and inadequately but that are also contradictory on a scientific level. First of all, since the introduction of aesthetics as a scientific concept around 1750, the applications through history have changed a great deal. The Greek word *aisthesis* means perception; art was discussed from that viewpoint by both Plato and Aristotle, even if they arrived at totally opposite conclusions. Plato criticized the mimetic character of art: art was just a copy of nature, which in its turn was a distorted, illusory picture of the real world, the true ideas that we are unable to grasp, due to our imperfect senses. Art, especially music, intoxicated our perceptions to the extent that it was to be forbidden or strictly regulated in the ideal state.

Aristotle, on the other hand, looked upon the limitations and expressions of art as something valuable for the individual and society. To imitate is amusing for both the artist and the spectator; to experience strong emotions in theater and music releases tensions and passions. Aristotle and Longinus gave a lot of advice as to how to bring about artistic effects, as did Horace, Boileau, Corneille, Pope, Diderot, Lessing, and many others after them.

In modern times, aesthetics became a branch of philosophy, an abstract discussion on the nature of art, beauty, and how aesthetic perceptions differ from other perceptions. In our century, the normative aspects, the discussion of aesthetic value, has diminished in academic circles. Instead, a development toward more objective distinctions has taken place, owing to the dominant influence of English and American aesthetics. After Wittgenstein, aesthetics had to find its boundaries and to restrict its applications. Recent aesthetics is often occupied with so-called speech acts, a rather formal analysis of different aesthetic concepts, normally disregarding specific works of art. Scientific aesthetics tries to categorize and systemize common features in art creation, experience, and criticism. To give one example, the American nominalist philosopher Nelson Goodman has in his book *Languages of Art* (1976) produced a most logical and coherent basis for an aesthetic terminology. As symptoms of the aesthetic he lists three basic characteristics: namely, syntactic density, semantic density, and syntactic repleteness. According to Goodman, density is constitutive for works of art; that is, the character of aesthetic objects as well as their corresponding experiences cannot be articulate, fixed, or explicitly denoted. All implications of aesthetic objects and experiences move in a glissando manner; no articulate steps, scales, or measurements in the perception capture anything significant, although all three features call for maximum sensitivity of discrimination. In Goodman's words:

> Syntactic and semantic density demand endless attention to determining character and referent. Syntactic repleteness distinguishes the more representational among semantically dense systems from the more diagrammatic, the less from the more schematic. Syntactic density is characteristic of nonlinguistic systems.

As a fourth and complimentary symptom of the aesthetic, Goodman proposes the feature that distinguishes exemplification from denotation; combined with density, this distinguishes showing from saying. So density, repleteness, and exemplification are earmarks of the aesthetic; articulateness, attenuation, and denotation earmarks of the nonaesthetic.

Symbolization, according to Goodman, is based on curiosity, the urge to know; what delights is discovery, and communication is secondary to the apprehension and formulation of what is to be communicated. Symbolization is to be judged fundamentally by how well it serves the cognitive purpose: by the delicacy of its discriminations and the aptness of its allusions; by the way it works in grasping, exploring, and informing the world; by how it analyzes, sorts, orders, and organizes; by how it participates in the making, manipulation, retention, and transformation of knowledge.

Man is a social animal, communication is a requisite for social intercourse, and symbols are media of communication. Dogs go on barking, and men go on symbolizing when there is no practical need, just because they cannot stop and because it is such fun.

It would appear by now that electronic music may be unusually apt to fulfill the requirements of an aesthetic object. There seem to be no limitations in density and repleteness; even the largest orchestra cannot deliver anything near the potential amount of acoustic information of electronic and computer music. How is it then that electronic music without extra ingredients normally is regarded as being emptied after just one or a few presentations?

Electronic pieces may be extremely complex and rich in musical
ideas, sounds, forms, and expressive details, yet there is seldom an
impulse to listen again and again. I have a feeling that this is also
true of people who are professionally occupied with electronic
music. Certainly everybody may have a couple of favorite electronic compositions that they listen to on several occasions. However, this seems to be the exception rather than the rule, whereas
we listen to other types of music repeatedly without much irrita-
tion.

These circumstances may not be fatal for an individual composer or a certain piece. To listen once can be quite satisfactory,
even an advantage. But that goes for other types of music as well,
without being a characteristic, regular feature. In electronic music
there are probably certain distinguishing qualities that hitherto
have prevented this music from establishing itself in musical society. General conservatism and ignorance do not provide a sufficient explanation, since we may encounter the same negative
attitudes among devoted specialists. Also, the novelty of electronic
music has become a less valid excuse for this nonacceptance or for
indifferent reactions.

If we assume that there are in fact some important elements in
electronic music that obstruct the urge within the listener to
explore and develop his apprehension of a piece, then that is not
to say that these elements are to be found in *all* electronic compositions or that they must always be a problem. But here we can
only discuss the subject theoretically; consequently we generalize,
approximate, and imply statistical middle-of-the-road ex-
emplifications.

In looking for problematic elements of electronic music in
general, we realize that the composer is confronted with his first
dilemma in deciding whether he should pay any attention at all to
these elements or not. That is no easy decision, since we always
have a tendency to break aesthetic rules, to go against logic, the
reasonable and promising, to experiment, to bypass the problems,
or search for the golden egg of absolute surprise. All this is an
integral part of creativity. As John Cage puts it, "Art is not about
being right." The technical complications and concessions in the
studio work invite sometimes notions of opposition even against
one's own interests. These cautious maneuvers may go unnoticed
by anyone but the composer—blunt anarchy or demonstrations
being more embarrassing but effective.

The seemingly most apparent aesthetic dilemma to consider is
the absence in electronic music of what we might call natural

references. Instrumental and vocal music are entirely based upon familiar references in all musical dimensions; abstract patterns as well as the expressive functions rest firmly on spatially and psychologically functioning orientation marks. Many of these references have been results of cultivation rather than given by nature. Well-tempered scales, regular rhythms, triadic harmony, instrument-making, and other important components of western music require habituation through centuries to become natural organic references. Even so, most of the widespread references in history have now been lost forever. Very few care that we listen to Josquin, Monteverdi, and Bach as if we had some idea what such highly specialized symbolization means. Stand-in references and interpretations, always being up-to-date and à la mode, of course are elegantly put together in concert program commentaries and on record covers.

In the introductions to electronic music pieces, however, it has become common to present references that the listener has no possibility of detecting. Composers often forget to differentiate between the obvious construction in the compositional procedure and the totally different construction—not reconstruction—made by the listener. Composing data and sense data in listening are far apart in the case of electronic music.

Despite terminology, electronic music has no natural connection to ordinary music whatsoever; its sound-material did not develop from traditional music and is consequently not from the beginning conceived with musical elements. It has an entirely different infrastructure; the relations between details in instrumental music cannot be directly compared with relations in electronic music. Instrumental and vocal music are what Roland Barthes calls "Musica Practica"; every instant is related to a physical reality: playing, capacities of instruments, expressive behavior, and an explicit interaction of people. This cannot be reproduced or transformed into classical electronic music. There remains perhaps only the alternative to build up references typical for electronic music. How can this be done?

It seems to me that general references with a more definite cognitive and emotive meaning are rather unlikely in electronic music in the foreseeable future. Electronic music is admittedly self-reflecting, but in too vague a sense: it sounds and behaves like electronic music, but that is not sufficient as an aesthetic reference for individual pieces. The basis for electronic music is a continuum in all parameters and respects. The parameters do not stop at natural points, as in traditional music; there are no scales, no given articulation, no footholds for discrimination in composition or listening. The alleged objectivity of electronic music turns into extreme subjectivity as soon as the tapes leave the studio.

Now, references and orientation marks do not necessarily have to be natural, universal, or preconceived. They can function as so-called conventional symbols; that is, they become agreed upon and accepted in a *singular* context. In theory, it is always possible to establish references in the framework of a certain composition or even a specific composer.

Any significant sound or gesture would be acceptable for such a purpose. Continuous references, such as drones or constant beats, will give relations for pitches, tempo, and durations; clear accents may give dynamic orientation. Small alterations in the references are not likely to destroy their functions, but a repetitive character must be regarded as essential. It is difficult to point out constructive, formative elements in modernistic music as a whole, so the more amorphous and inarticulate the material, the more obvious and clearly defined the intended references.

Related to this is another dilemma in electronic music: how to relate foreground elements to a background, or even how to establish a background. This is similar to information and redundancy in information theory. It is believed that good perception results from a certain predominance of redundancy over the new and the original. Maximum redundancy means having experienced something to the point where one gets bored. Maximum information means that we have no repertory to work the signals. A well-functioning balance between these factors results in classic art and music, a disturbed balance, which historically alternates, might result in manneristic art.

Foreground and background are elements noted in Gestalt psychology. Gestalt psychology maintains that our nervous system has been developed according to biological conditions offered by the outer world. A gestalt and a reference may not be the same thing: the gestalt does not have to be reference, but the reference must be a gestalt. So, to consider references in a piece means to realize the fundamentals of gestalt theory. In turn, lots of consequences will leave their marks on the compositions. A piece may begin with an exposition of references that will not be varied as in instrumental motif-compositions, but nonetheless a certain concession to a more pedagogic and less sophisticated form and presentation of materials will be difficult to avoid.

This dilemma can be dealt with in the same way as Stockhausen, Berio, and others have done. By utilizing relatively well-known musical objects or human interjections as references, their electronic sound patterns can move rather freely and still make sense for the listener. As a matter of fact, very little, just a tiny reminder of something outside the electronic music world—or "ghetto" as Xenakis calls it—gives a feeling of identity. Electronic music as a genre becomes a macrogestalt or macroreference, no matter what it sounds like. Besides, the more realistic musical object, be it a fragment of folk music, a street noise, or whatever, gets a new interpretation in the context of electronic music. It is certainly a reliable and simple technique, the dilemma being that it is not anymore a very inventive and creative formal idea.

Another dilemma to consider is whether or not to build electronic pieces with scales of different kinds. This becomes a more acute question in our day of synthesizers and keyboard inputs. In principle, we are dealing here more with the aesthetic of live electronic music, even if keyboard pieces are not performed directly at concerts but produced in studios. It is a difference in the concept of composition more than a remarkable difference in the final piece. The composer's approach toward the musical material is highly affected by the presence of keyboards, computer terminals, or other decisive inputs in comparison to the more amorphous handling of knobs, faders, potentiometers, etc. Keyboards and numbers may give clear references in the composing process, which does not mean that the piece is referential for the listener. If scales or similar characteristics are perceived, it would be difficult not to think of instrumental music with electronic means. As we all know, this is exactly the easy way to popularity.

In the last few years, a lot of research has been accumulated in music psychology, neurology, experimental hearing, and other related disciplines. The work at IRCAM may result in important guidelines after the initial problems that have occurred there. It has already been established as a tradition that particularly electronic music should stay in close contact with what is going on in science and technology. Electronic music is definitely not allowed to be stupid, naive, and sentimental. It is tacitly expected to be the sounding science of music, unless it belongs to the other big category: electronic impressionism. It is natural to link electronic music to science and technology, since all of its sources and possible transformations are dependent on achievements in those fields. Composers may feel that they have to give something back and be related to technicians. Nevertheless, further extramusical pressure is put on electronic music composers. They have to keep up, more or less superficially, with developments in many fields.

To balance that with an expanding insight into musical questions gives rise to an enormous dilemma, which is probably not as strongly felt among instrumental music composers. The real background for this difference is perhaps a tendency in electronic music to be concerned with the external, materialistic world, while instrumental music is more devoted to established existential and formal subjects. It is difficult to communicate expressive nuances with electronic means; it is easier to stay in the technical atmosphere with relevant symbolization and related topics. The medium is very much the message: electronic music is also most convincing when confined to its own limited territory and not trying to imitate traditional music qualities. Keeping the previous discussion on reference and gestalt in mind, perhaps it is a major fault in electronic music to overestimate its aesthetic capacity.

The propagandistic talk in the early years of electronic music made investments and other contributions possible, but they could hardly be paid back with artistic results as soon as they were implicitly understood. The "limitless possibilities" shrank to a small repertoire of clichés and familiar timbres. Results in electronic music can now hardly overtake exaggerated expectations. Electronic music is caught in the rat race. New investments require bigger promises, computers and other equipment become faster and more effective, the composers are chased by new computer programs and by new installations in an accelerating tempo. It has become, as Stockhausen recently pointed out, very difficult to go *deeply* into musical problems—something that produces vast aesthetic implications and dilemmas.

One well-known effect of the association to science and technology is the widespread use of adventurous applications. For instance, quoting Leonard B. Meyer: "It is an inexcusable error to equate acoustical phenomena with qualitiative experiences. The former are abstract scientific concepts, the latter are psychological perceptions. There is no one-to-one relationship between an acoustical event and its concomitant perceptual experience." The primary dilemma in this context is whether or not to concentrate on scientific concepts in electronic music composition. Granted, there are many questions and experiments that can be effectively carried out by electronic studio facilities—do they so often have to be covered by the sensuous veils of music? In the long run, this ambivalence may turn out to be negative for electronic music as a whole.

Unfortunately, there seems to be no easy way out of this dilemma.

The transport of scientific models to aesthetic characteristics is as old as art and science themselves. A continuous accommodation is taking place. In our industrialized society, where the large majority of intellectuals are occupied with science and technology instead of the arts and humanities, as in former days, a shift of the focusing point for ideas and for the creation of forms is somehow bound to come. If and when this transformation is more accentuated, I strongly believe that the intermediary role of the artist in electronic music will decline in the near future. Specialized programmers will be able to perform complex structures, sounds, and forms that are out of reach for the average electronic music composer. Self-generating composing machines will deliver acceptable pieces of music in any requested style, including those with a charming human touch. Xenakis was very right in saying: "Music is by nature abstract. Therefore it could be the first of all the arts to unite scientific thinking with artistic creativity."

Maybe it is no dilemma for the contemporary electronic music composer whether or not to support and accelerate this development. The reason I bring it up here is that whatever direction the composer chooses, the aesthetic consequences are comprehensive. Anything like a scientifically-conceived music, expositions of models, and their rational interactions, is, of course, contrary to the definitions of an aesthetic object as formulated earlier by Nelson Goodman. The rational treatment of sounds and structures, when also perceived by the listeners, tends to what he lists as non-aesthetic: articulation, attenuation, and denotation. Music is no more subjected to an endlessly dense discrimination and interpretation; it becomes an object for correct or incorrect understanding, a formula of sounds with one single solution. Emotive reactions may be regarded as irrelevant and suppressed by listeners. Dynamic elements may disappear or may have to be reinterpreted totally. Perhaps composers avoid emphasizing such problems in order not to lose audiences—just as modernist artists have often declared that it was not necessary to realize the complexity and differentiation of their works (you only have to listen)—as if the aesthetic attitude would not have been entirely different in the pieces were they merely meant to be listened to!

It is certainly most legitimate to imitate and make models of artificial and abstract phenomena just as much as of human feelings, nature sounds, or the like. In principle, aesthetics would not treat even works by machines or random generators in any other way than it would treat those composed and realized by man. Whatever is presented as an aesthetic object and accepted by the world as such as possible to analyze, categorize, and criticize in an aesthetic terminology. The American philosopher George Dickie maintains, however, that a work of art has to be an *artifact*, which has had conferred upon it the status of candidate for appreciation by some person or institution. Now, it is an interesting question whether self-regulating, cybernetic machines produce artifacts or not. I think the answer will be yes in not too many years.

A lot of what has been said here boils down to one fundamental characteristic of electronic music: its dependence on external elements, both as references and subjects. The extreme neutrality of its apparatus requires to be filled with a content that hardly can be offered by purely musical means. Besides—as already mentioned—"musical" elements are those born out of the physical aspects of making music with the body and its nervous system. Indeed, preelectronic music has also been highly dependent on extramusical elements, as the basic physical language is never sufficient; but such elements have dissolved through a long tradition into what we now regard as natural musical expressions and symbols. We encounter important aesthetic dilemmas in electronic music just because so little has amalgamated with it in its relatively short time of existence.

About ten years ago, Herbert Brün wrote: "In order that the composer's choice may be significant and carry a meaning, the relationship between the chosen and the eliminated possibilities must be perceived."

It is difficult to see how this demand can be fulfilled in such an aesthetically continuous medium as electronic music, where there is no natural beginning or end, no upper or lower limits, no steps or recognizable levels to choose among, no directions, no audible distinctions between the man-made (personal) and the machine-made (impersonal). So, perhaps the perceived choices made by the composer are something that has to be abandoned as an ideal of electronic music. What has been estimated as a token of artistic quality in traditional music may have no place in electronic music. This is not to be regretted too much, I think. What are obvious weaknesses in electronic music as compared to instrumental music or even musique concrète could here be judged as strengths and distinctive features. The dilemma of electronic music composers is to an extent the fact that they are composers with one half of the brain rooted in traditional music and its totally different nature. The necessary paradigm shift has not yet taken place: we are still in the state of anomalies, as Thomas Kuhn would have formulated it. According to him, a new generation is a requisite for an old paradigm to be buried. Above all, earlier habits control perception very strongly. In 1949, Bruner and Postman conducted experiments with playing cards, which demonstrated that even if the exposition time of false cards in a certain well-known context was multiplied forty times, people accepted them as correct cards. Expectations of the normal prevent the discovery of anomalies. We cannot expect or even hope for important changes in listening attitudes for our own purposes.

Electronic music, a child of the cathode-ray tube and transistor more than a Stravinsky and a Webern, may provoke a paradigm shift in the history and perception of music. In case the shift will not occur in the long run, serious aesthetic dilemmas will prevail for such classic electronic music that is not based on playing, imitative synthesis, or that exists as a part of other media, such as video or film.

It is doubtful if the more abstract form of electronic music has enough social impact to implement a major change in music preference. Indeed, the intimate contacts with science and technology bring prestige and logic as well as positivistic pats on the shoulders. But if classic electronic music is carried by an ideology that runs parallel to the *Weltanschauung* of science—something that many studios (or "research centers") already ahdere to—it nevertheless leaves other socially important functions of music for other genres to exploit.

Anarchistic qualities, absurdity, entertainment, expressionism, etc., do not fit very well in the laboratory—not to mention those artists who are devoted to such things. This raises a new dilemma for some composers: how will it be possible to integrate more traditional and nonscientific elements into a rationalistic atmosphere? It is not quite as simple as Xenakis puts it: "Content, in art is to convey information." The same information may have opposite aesthetic rules to follow. Art is a qualitative matter, aesthetically very different from what information theory calls "source," "transmitter," and "receiver." So the integration of antagonistic, contrasting elements, such as scientific and nonscientific concepts in a piece, is a much more delicate affair.

Today we notice a tendency in electronic music to deal with sound, timbre, and harmony rather than structures. This demonstrates a specialization for which electronic music is very suitable, perhaps even superior to instrumental music. Electronic pop groups show a similar evolution. Certainly, we face a dilemma here as well. Electronic music has an impressive potential in the attractiveness of its sounds. Spectrums and coloristic nuances may have an unprecedented purity. To be unaffected by this as a composer requires a very strong character. To work with structures, on the other hand, means to move the attention from the sensuous medium, the sounds, to relations and processes. This seems much more demanding.

The negative development of the western industrialized societies in the last few years may be a reason for the tendency toward a static, amorphous style. Structures and positivistic compositions are perhaps symbolic of an optimistic era. A balance between these opposite approaches to music within a composition results in classicism; a disproportion produces aesthetic mannerisms. Of course, this is not to say that classic art is to be preferred. Preferences are matters for artists and the public, not for the aesthetician. However, aesthetics with all its accumulated research can be in a position to observe tendencies and consequences that the more specialized artists and critics may not be able to see. Aesthetics can offer little help in the dilemmas that torture so many artists nowadays; it cannot alter the development of art forms, no matter how destructive they may seem to the academic eye, which can compare parallels in a historic context. Aesthetics can serve as criticism: artistic concepts as well as disputes among art critics are sometimes quite unreasonable. Aesthetics can give warnings and point to the dangerous effect of exaggerated mannerisms in electronic music, for instance. But it cannot influence artists against their will with intellectual arguments. Nor can aesthetics solve artistic dilemmas but only try to sort them out and perhaps inform how similar dilemmas were dealt with by artists in earlier years.

Electronic music is aesthetically problematic to an extent that has probably not been realized before. Also, electronic music is very difficult to discuss in academic aesthetic terms, since aesthetics is more concerned with philosophic analyses of personal artifacts lacking many technological implications. Its position outside the framework of a regular musical tradition and effects creates a number of dilemmas for the individual composer and listener—a fact previously unheard of in history. The future possibilities for an abstract electronic music, not just models or automatic deliveries, are very uncertain. But the intuitive and creative way artists resolve dilemmas may very possibly lead to totally unexpected combinations of aesthetic elements.

Aesthetic Direction in Electronic Music

Jon H. Appleton
DARTMOUTH COLLEGE

This article was written and published when I was a graduate student at the University of Oregon. Although a quarter century has passed, many of the aesthetic issues raised are still pertinent as well as being of historical interest.

Of all the arts, music seems to have been most affected by the scientific revolution of the last decade. Not only have composers seen their colleagues discard traditional musical structures, they have seen the "imagination" threatened by the computer and the orchestra made obsolete by the sound studio.

Within universities in the United States, departments and schools of music are beginning to accept the reality of electronic music as a serious compositional medium. When referring to electronic music I mean music composed by using electronic instruments and concrète sounds by living composers and by computers.

The organization of new sound studios does not mean that there has been a universal acceptance of this music within the music profession itself. Two recent articles in professional publications, entitled "The Fallacy of Mathematical Composition"[1] and "The Avant-Gardist—A Product of Process,"[2] seem to be an accurate representation of the feelings of most musicians toward this new music. The authors, Joshua Missal and Hubert Lamb, are quick to condemn any compositional techniques touched by mathematical or scientific considerations. The articles reveal an abundance of prejudice and little understanding of the contemporary scene. Typically enough, they have confused totally serialized compositions with works that use the twelve-tone row merely as one of many unifying techniques. The authors have failed to differentiate between electroacoustic music, which is composed by a computer's random selection of tones, and music that has been artfully constructed by a composer much in the same way he might compose a piece for orchestra. Lamb does not "believe that the procedures of the avant-garde produce music now; nor . . . given a long era of refinement and development, that they will produce music in the future." He further considers composers of this music as "victims of this seductive technology" and that their work is "simply not to be evaluated on music's terms."

Lamb, Missal, their colleagues, and the majority of the musically educated population have been led to their antagonistic opinions by the seemingly large amount of material that must be assimilated before there can be any appreciation of the possibilities of electronic music. Above all, they have been confused because aesthetic considerations have been obscured by scientific ones. The purposes of this paper are to show that aesthetic and scientific considerations can be separated and to outline some basic aesthetic criteria for the study and composition of electronic music. There is no reason why the listener must respond in the unfortunate posture of ignorance.

There is little cogent writing on the aesthetics of today's music. Only Leonard B. Meyer has attempted to analyze seriously problems of the contemporary musical aesthetic. Since the publication of *Emotion and Meaning in Music* in 1956, Meyer has revised and expanded many of his ideas in articles, of which two are pertinent here.[3] In an article entitled "The End of the Renaissance?" Meyer reviews the present avant-garde movement in music with reference to painting, literature, and philosophy.[4] He demonstrates that the fundamental character of music prior to the avant-garde was "teleological," viz. orientation toward a goal. This is opposed to the aesthetic of the avant-garde, where ". . . the audience should not attempt to choose, even unconsciously, among alternative possibilities for continuation. We ought to remain detached; seeing, hearing and observing the objective series of empirical events," a philosophy that Meyer calls "anti-teleological." These definitions may accurately be applied to the originators of electronic music in Germany, one of whom, Herbert Eimert, writes:

> Alone among the twelve-tone composers, Anton Webern conceived the row nonsubjectively, so that to a certain extent it functioned

externally. Seen from Schoenberg's viewpoint this would be like cutting the threads of life in music; a silence, a dumbness, an end. In truth, this end is our beginning.

And later in the article,

> It does not seem out of place here to question the possible objectivity of music. . . . Webern restricted his music to interval and single note [sic] and composed structures which are not in the traditional sense developed in a continuum. . . . Only in electronic music has the real sense of these developments been realized. . . . It is not that music can be composed by electronic means "too"; in the contemporary phase of music only one way can be seen of determining the compositional situation, that is: "after Webern," the situation resulting from the discovery of the *single* note.[5]

The coeditors of *Die Reihe,* Herbert Eimert and Karlheinz Stockhausen, are among the originators of electronic music and are still the most influential composer-theorists in the field. Postwar Germany, uprooted from its traditions, financed by the United States, has apparently led the electronic "anti-teleological" school to a point of no discussion.

What Eimert is saying here is that the ordering of sounds is no longer important, that rather we should direct our attention to the individual tone, which is many times more significant in an electronic environment than in traditional music. How this is accomplished is explained in great detail so that one is nearly lost in a forest of technical terms and scientific jargon. This the trusting reader supposes to be the proof of his case. In fact,

> If we boil down *Die Reihe* to see wht solid content it has, we find first that the amount of valid scientific material vaporizes immediately; next, the technical jargon boils off, taking quite a time to do so, since there is so much of it; and finally, what remains is a microscopic residuum consisting of nothing more than a mystical belief in numerology as the fundamental basis for music.[6]

It would be fair to say that some special knowledge and vocabulary are necessary to the discussion of electronic music. However, one suspects that by compounding esoteric terminology with a pedantic aesthetic, the Cologne school has frightened the emperor into seeing his new clothes. Fortunately, the Cologne studios under the direction of Eimert and Stockhausen represent only one of many schools of electronic composition.

L. A. Hiller, Jr., of the University of Illinois (now at the State University of New York at Buffalo—ED.), leads the field of electronic music in the United States. His book, *Experimental Music* (1959), is still the standard reference work in a rapidly changing field. Hiller has devoted the first part of the book to a discussion of some of the aesthetic problems of electronic music, especially that which is produced by a computer.[7] The computer is used to produce music following certain instructions, which are "programmed" for the individual computer. The *Illiac Suite* is one example of Hiller's work with the computer.(See Hiller, "Electronic Sonata," below, for another example. ED.) The suite was composed by giving the computer specific instructions as to pitch, intervals, voice leading, etc., and within the scope of these instructions letting the computer select at random the notes of the composition. The work, scored for string quartet, is characterized by a monotonous texture and might best be described as directionless. More often the computer has been used to "compose" music for electronic instruments.

Hiller has acknowledged the importance of Meyer's earlier writings and recognized the limitations of completely random music.

> Restricting the number of choices should tend to increase the "meaningfulness" of messages. Thus the most diffuse types of music are produced on the average when successive note selection is permitted to be completely random. As we shall see, music of this type is rather easily generated in a computer and *forms the basic substance from which we must fashion more characteristic structures.*[8]

Hiller commits himself herewith to the teleological school of thought. He is attempting to compose meaningful structures by recognizing the necessity of predictability and choice. As Meyer says, "Communication requires that the artist imagine or predict how others—the audience—will interpret and respond to the . . . sounds he produces."[9] At the same time, however, Hiller wants to use the computer for the random selection of his materials. His error is quite simply that of wanting to have his cake and eat it too.

One cannot criticize a work more harshly than to call it dull, and the *Illiac Suite* is dull because it satisfies neither aesthetic. Were the composition completely random there would always exist the chance, remote as it is, that the work might have some meaningful relationships or what musicians often call "life"; were it composed in its entirety by a human imagination, then it would have a better chance of being meaningful. In *Experimental Music* Hiller asks his audience to appreciate the *Illiac Suite* because of the truly clever and complex compositional process that produced it. Alan Walker points out that

> . . . we do not properly understand much of the music of our own time and we compensate for this unique situation in words. The amount of literature dealing with contemporary music is almost equal in bulk to the music itself. It is the rule rather than the exception to find new works accompanied at their first performance by technical essays of varying lengths and obscurity, often written by the composer himself.[10]

In the world of electronic music one receives the impression that most composers would rather have you listen to their explications than to their music.

Perhaps recognizing the limitations of the *Illiac Suite* and music of this kind, Hiller turned his attention to electronic music for the theater. In 1959 he produced a score for John Leckel's *Blue is the Antecedent of It* and in 1960, for Christopher Newton's *Cuthbert Bound*. Both plays represent a new direction in theater that might be described as postdadaistic. Hiller's move from the most rigidly controlled music to a freely associative kind of theater music truly revealed his limitations. His scores for the productions mentioned above are careless conglomerations of concrète and electronically produced sounds. The individual sounds are carefully selected to reflect the text, but their variety and unrelatedness perceived by the listener in a short space are staggering and confusing. The consistent lack of meaning between dramatic events on the stage creates an unusual sense of its own. The scores, however, offer such plethora of aural stimuli that the audience is unable to tell whether discontinuity is the objective of the compositions or the result of the inexperience of the individual listener.

Morton Subotnick, of the California Institute of the Arts, has created much the same effect in his "opera," *A Theatre Piece After Sonnet No. 47 of Petrarch*. On either side of the stage, music pours from speakers as a girl in white slowly walks around a stage filled with burning candles. The music consists of a recorded spoken voice, a piano piece by Liszt, a viola solo, concrète and electronic sounds blended into a thirty-minute collage. There is a definite relation between the music and the action on stage. A man in overalls opens the piano lid just as the Liszt comes over the speakers. Overlooking the damage done to Petrarch and Liszt, Subotnick has created a theater piece of very low quality. Both the score with its abrupt and dissociated sounds and the nearly inactive action seem designed as accompaniments. Neither part, however, is worthy of the accompaniment of the other.

Both Hiller and Subotnick, in their theater compositions, have created antiteleological music even though it was not their intention to do so. These gentlemen have imagination and craftsmanship at their disposal, but they have been unable to fulfill the expectations raised by the new medium.

Inherent in electronic music are astounding new possibilities for sound production and manipulation. However, composers and students of this new music will not overcome public resistance to their work until they realize that aural stimulation is not an end in itself. The listener can appreciate new sounds presented for their own sake only for short periods of time.

One does not expect that the sonata form, a tone row, or any previously successful organizational technique will work in this new context. But because aural sensations are new and complex, composers will have to bring continuity and structure to the new music. Artistic perception is not merely enhanced by form; it is dependent on it. Theodore Meyer Greene states that

> . . . although the artistic form of a work of art is the *peculiar* locus of its artistic quality, this form is not merely an end in itself but also, and essentially, a means, in fact the only means, whereby the artist can express himself and communicate his ideas to others.[11]

Random procedures of organization are justly suspect in traditional music (i.e., string quartets, etc.) and perhaps only time can bestow the final verdict. If randomness is suspect in a familiar context, how can composers hope to communicate when they use randomness in a world of new sound? It is the responsibility of composers to rely on their *music* to communicate to the listener. There is no reason why electronic music cannot communicate if the composer will remain faithful to his art and compose what he wants others to hear. His explanations are not and will never be part of the musical experience.

Notes

1. Joshua Missal, "The Fallacy of Mathematical Composition," *American Music Teacher* 12 (1962): 25.

2. Hubert Lamb, "The Avant-Gardist—A Product of Process," *Music Journal* 22, no. 1 (January 1964): 85.

3. See "Some Remarks on Value and Greatness in Music," *The Journal of Aesthetics and Art Criticism* 17, no. 4 (1959): 32; and "Meaning in Music and Information Theory," *The Journal of Aesthetics and Art Criticism* 15, no. 4 (1957): 46.

4. "The End of the Renaissance?" *Hudson Review* 16, no. 2 (1963): 181.

5. "What is Electronic Music?" *Die Reihe: Electronic Music* (London: Universal Edition, 1955).

6. John Backus, "*Die Reihe*—A Scientific Evaluation," *Perspectives of New Music* (Fall 1962): 160 f.

7. For a current discussion, see M. V. Mathews, "The Digital Computer as a Musical Instrument," *Science* 142 (November 1963): 553.

8. L. A. Hiller and Leonard M. Issacson, *Experimental Music* (New York: McGraw-Hill, 1959), p. 31.

9. Meyer, "The End of the Renaissance," p. 181.

10. Alan Walker, *A Study in Musical Analysis* (London: Barrie and Rockliff, 1962), p. 16.

11. Theodore Meyer Greene, *The Arts and the Art of Criticism* (Princeton: Princeton University Press, 1952), p. 123.

The Development of Personal Compositional Style

Barry Schrader
CALIFORNIA INSTITUTE OF THE ARTS, VALENCIA

"Style is the dress of thoughts," said Lord Chesterfield. Most people would probably agree, for we often tend to think of the style of a particular work of art as those obvious qualities which allow us to pigeonhole it. But the style of a work of music goes beyond the superficial and tells us something not only of the time and place of its creation, it can also reveal something of the personality of the composer.

In my own musical cosmology, style is the fourth, in order of increasing complexity, of what I believe to be the five main areas of information:

General Areas of Musical Information

    I. Dimensions of Musical Materials
   II. Structure
  III. Compositional Procedure
      A. Musical
      B. Translational
   IV. Style
      A. Historical/Geographical
      B. Personal
    V. Kinetic Process
      A. Perception
      B. Teleology

These areas are, of course, interrelated, which is why I mention them all here, in a brief article devoted to only one of them.

Style is the name we give to particular combinations of elements over a range of time sufficiently wide for them to become perceptually relevant. The period of time may be historical, or, for the kinetic arts, within a given work or group of works. In music, for example, we speak of the baroque style, the Italian baroque style, and of Vivaldi's style. Style analysis is usually only cursorily included in music curriculums. Perhaps this is because it is a less quantifiable area than structure or procedure, being the result of combinations of elements and therefore more gestalt-oriented. It may also be a less popular area of investigation because it requires some attention in listening and opens up the area of the perception of music.

Historical styles are usually presented in neat codifications as statistically culled quantifications of features of works in a particular time and place. The problem with this is twofold: performance practice is often overlooked or misunderstood, and details seem to become blurred or lost in direct proportion to their distance in time.[1] How many of us could aurally distinguish among Gallic, Ambrosian, Mozarabic, and Celtic chant styles were we able to hear them as originally performed? I suspect that these problems with the understanding of historical styles in general have led to some misconceptions about contemporary styles. Almost everyone will say, for example, that there is no longer a "common practice," or people will refer to "the" or "a common period." This strikes me as a kind of arrogance by definition. The use of a particular tonal system usually indicated by "common practice" was certainly not universal at any time in the past and is used by composers today. Furthermore, I suspect that there are many stylistic niceties and differences among all past musical styles that have been lost in the shuffle of time or relegated to unimportance. The use of style names has always been problematic, and "romanticism" makes no more sense when applied to music than does "minimalism."[2]

Common practices and styles have always existed and continue to exist today; they are not universal, but they never have been. Today there seems to be a large number of practices, however, so many that they appear to be common styles of only relatively small communities. But this perception may be due more to the fact that we are now aware of details that will be lost in the process of historification than to the actual existence of many distinctly different schools of practice.

More than twenty years ago, Leonard Meyer suggested, in *Music, the Arts, and Ideas,* that contemporary art music might have reached a period of stasis in which all styles, past and present, coexist in a Sargasso sea of nondevelopment. Clearly, this has not been the case. There have been very large stylistic movements that have come and gone in the twentieth century, and it is now possible to look at the serial and chance styles of the 1950s and 1960s with somewhat the same attitude of codification that has been given to the *ars nova*. In fact, recent musical styles may be even more "common" than anything in past western culture because so many people have been participating in them.[3]

Historical or period styles are always in flux, as are the rate and degree of their change. The notion of style periods that come from name designations quickly become self-referential and somewhat artificial. Historical styles are group styles, a compendium of different personal styles. If, at a given time, Composer 1 does A and C, Composer 2 does B and C, and Composer 3, C and D; C becomes a determining factor in defining their collective style Σ, while A, B and D are indicative of personal styles. If, later on, other composers start to do C, they will probably be classified as Σ composers. Subclassifications may be discerned in that composers may be doing AC, BC, or ED, and so we would have the schools $\Sigma 1$, $\Sigma 2$, and $\Sigma 3$. Suddenly, someone decides to do A, C, and F; an innovation occurs, eventually A and C are abandoned, and a new movement, Ω, arrives. So we see that historical period or group styles are really dependent on personal styles. But where did A, B, C, D, and F come from? What determined the initial limitation of selection of stylistic elements for these composers? How does personal style develop?

I believe that personal style develops in three progressive and interactive ways: through external experience, by self-comprehension, and in the synthesis of both of these. At any given moment, one is the sum total of one's experience, and this includes the ability to process it. Learning is accomplished initially by imitation and by trial and error. Young composers naturally select from what is present as the range of possibilities. Of vital importance is the music one hears at a very early age; from this is learned not only beginning aesthetics, but also the very act of how to listen to music. Also important is the music one performs and the instrument one plays.[4] To a large extent, this early musical experience is visceral, not cogitative. Much of this kind of experience is common to a large proportion of society, but only a very small percentage go beyond it.

Trained composers, especially composers of art music, enter a second stage of external experience: formalized education. Unlike the first stage, this is largely a mental process. Young composers are taught large doses of the first three categories of musical information that I mentioned earlier: information about musical dimensions (pitch, dynamics, rhythm, timbre, etc.); musical structure; and compositional procedure (harmony, counterpoint, serial technique, electroacoustic music systems, computer music programs, etc.). One of the main reasons that these areas are so emphasized is that they are easily quantifiable; thus they may be codified, tested, repeated, and formally manipulated. In what I believe is a misconception and misappropriation of ideas from the empirical sciences, quantification in music has been thought of as delineating the atomic entities of sound from which the molecular structure of music may be fashioned by mere procedures of combination. It is as though apprentice chefs were taught in great detail the properties of, say, the one hundred statistically most important culinary ingredients and then told that cooking consisted of creating combinations of these elements, and, furthermore, that the quality of the results should be judged not by their taste but by the preconceived elegance of their formulation.

While a knowledge of musical structure and procedure of the past (and it can only be of the past) are important and necessary to the composer's craft and sophistication, it will usually not allow for the development of a well-defined personal style. Perhaps for this reason, most composers do not get beyond this first stage of stylistic development. Their personal styles, therefore, are essentially reflection and imitations of their experiences. These composers may be great craftsmen in what they do, but they will probably never develop highly individualistic styles. To be sure, they do have individual styles, but these consist largely of things that are common to many other composers.

Contemporary composers of art music are often quick to negatively criticize popular composers for being imitative of whatever is currently fashionable. It seems to me, however, that the main difference between composers who intuitively imitate what they hear and those who consciously imitate what they are taught is what it is they are imitating. Perhaps this accounts for the fact that the majority of compositions, or of almost anything, is not very interesting.

In order to develop a distinctive compositional style, I believe that a composer must, knowingly or not, enter the next stages of development. The areas of self-comprehension and the synthesis of internal and external experience are closely related. They both require an intimate involvement with the perception of music as an aural kinetic process, not merely as the result or representation of procedures controlling specified quantities. It may be true that all perceived musical experience is reducible to procedural and quantitative information; were that the case, however, it would only be true for past events, since it is not possible to thoroughly analyze that which has not happened. Furthermore, the system of measurement of quantification would always have to be proven relevant in accurately and meaningfully relating human perception; this is perhaps not impossible, but it is certainly difficult. More important than quantitative information itself is how it is arranged. I believe we perceive music in terms of gestalts. While these gestalts can be analyzed for their components, these are always secondary to the whole, since it is there that the musical idea is embodied.

As composers develop, if they do develop, they begin to hear things in their own music that appeal to them in a special way. They find ideas, gestalts, which perhaps they were not aware of before but somehow seem to reappear in their work. They try to understand and analyze these ideas and eventually to capitalize on them. These musical ideas, these gestalts, become the basis of a developed and distinct personal compositional style. At the same time, I believe, an ongoing synthesis develops with regard to both the internal and external world; information about oneself and about the outside world becomes processed into something new; knowledge and acceptance allow for realization. In a way, perhaps, one goes back to that early stage where musical perception was formed, but now, instead of learning how to listen, the need is to understand how one listens.

Finally, I believe an attitude develops, at least to some degree, that the musical idea proceeds its delineation. Composition becomes not a matter of combination but of deciding what one needs and how one must deal with it in order to achieve a particular goal. Music is a form of communication. Perhaps in the distant past what we now refer to as music was initially and inseparably linked with human movement (including human imitation of nonhuman movement) and vocal inflection. If this were the case, communication would have been fairly direct and obvious. One can easily see the connection here to the two most important communicative aspects of performance: the representational quality of gesture and the mechanical relationship between action and result.[5] But the physical performance aspects of music are now less important to communication than they once were, thanks to recordings and the general field of electroacoustic music. In listening experiences devoid of physical performance, one tends to concentrate on the actual sound of the music, the area of primary concern for most composers.[6] Here one finds what Meyer calls the "embodied" information of music, what I consider to be the gestalts that are abstract only in the sense that they are not tangible. These are ideas and they do communicate, but only to the degree that they are perceptually relevant and reveal teleology. Composers who have developed distinctive styles will, I find, communicate these ideas in their works.

One last brief comment: composers who do develop strong personal style seem to do so, as a rule, rather than earlier in their careers. I suspect that this is because a great deal of experience and work is necessary for this to happen.

And so I believe that personal compositional style is an extremely important part of what is eventually and historically considered valuable in music. Through personal style, composers relate to others something of themselves and their perceptions of life. Music, like the other arts, is, after all, about us.

Notes

1. Recorded works of electroacoustic music, particularly studio compositions, may, for the first time in history, allow for the opportunity to hear music as the composer intended. More than merely recorded performances, they are in most cases the considered and final decisions of their creators. This has begun to change, however, since computer music systems now easily allow for the repetition and alteration of works without ever reaching the traditional sound recording stage.

2. I suppose that we, as a race, continue to believe that we do not truly understand anything or feel secure with it until we can name it. Usually, however, it is not the creators of art that classify it.

A few years ago, I was asked to write an article on "minimalism" in music. After I thought about it for a while, I realized that I did not really know what was meant by the term. I researched the development of the movement in the art world, where the term was first applied, and failed to see how it easily referred to much music. Then I decided to ask several other composers what they thought the term meant. I discovered that not only was there no concensus of opinion, but that most of the composers considered to be "minimalists" by others rejected the appropriation of the term for themselves. As a result, I declined to write the article, realizing that to do so would require not so much reporting on a movement as creating one.

3. Perhaps styles come and go more quickly than before, but this is not entirely clear to me.

4. I have often thought that my own love of thick musical textures and very long envelopes is related to my early experiences playing large pipe organs.

5. A simple example of this is a percussionist forcefully striking tympani. The gesture of the action itself represents and communicates strength and power, and perhaps aggression, among other things. The mechanical cause-and-effect relationship between this action and the sound it produces is easily perceived and understood. It is, I believe, through these physical and visual actions that sighted people learned to relate to music in the past, and from which a great deal of communication was achieved.

6. Music that is primarily or solely about sound, i.e., that is not performance music, does not play well in nineteenth-century style concert/theater environments. "Loudspeaker music" does not belong in a proscenium setting any more than dance belongs on radio.

Part 2
Digital Electroacoustic Music: Problems and Questions

Computer Music Warmware:
The Human Perspective

Robin Julian Heifetz

I am a composer. With one exception, I have composed only electroacoustic music since 1977. In order to explain why this is the compositional milieu in which I choose to function, I must address a very profound psychological need. I can sit at home in my study, with score-paper, pencil and other necessary implements, attempting to compose a work for orchestra (I must add here that this is a task I have successfully undertaken in the past on more than one occasion). Unfortunately, in this context I am not really dealing with music itself but with dots, lines and other symbols that serve to represent my musical ideas—to suggest otherwise would be clearly nonsensical.

I wish to present an appropriate analogy from the plastic arts. Imagine a sculptor with clay: he sees it, touches it, and fondles it. When I compose music, I also need to touch and fondle my material. This sensual, interactive quality, so lacking in the compositional act of instrumental and vocal music, is a principal feature of both analog and digital electroacoustic media and the principal reason for my dedicated involvement in this field of endeavor.

In this special environment, my senses are aroused as never before. My musical appetites are indulged, and I do not walk away hungry and emaciated as I might if I were sitting at home writing dots and lines. I do not wish to convey that one cannot derive sufficient nourishment while engaged in the act of composing instrumental and vocal music, that I am given to the unrestrained indulging of my appetites, or that I remain unmoved after listening to more conventional media but rather that I am experiencing a frenzy of poetic inspiration and rapturous delight for the first time in my career, and I need not apologize to those opposed to contemporary modes of musical expression who feel compelled to describe sensuality and the exaltation that results as something not in accordance with the propriety of "accepted" musical behavior.

These wretched souls react in this manner because composers involved today in electroacoustic music—and especially in computer music (which is my area of specialization)—suffer from a serious malady whose pathology can be observed in the tendency to focus attention almost exclusively upon technological rather than musical matters. As this prevailing tendency invariably saps music of its potency and beauty, then why do these individuals adhere so perversely to an approach that cannot possibly satisfy aesthetic requirements or exhibit taste, discriminating judgment, and musical sensitivity?

When we speak about computer music, the word "computer" functions grammatically as a qualifier—that is, we are not talking about musical computers, because computers are not musical—in fact, computers are defined as artificial intelligence systems, which means that they are stupid as well. This suggests that only composers are disposed to creativity, and computers are unquestionably as dumb and as wanting in artistic imagination as any concert-grand piano.

The major cause of this malady is the fact that many colleagues simply think otherwise. The adamant refusal to acknowledge this state of affairs can be observed when they refer to their works as "computer-generated." It is not possible to sidestep the undeniable truth: compositions are *not* computer-generated—they are composer-generated! When a composer writes an orchestral work, he does not refer to it as "orchestra-generated." The term "generated" requires as a necessary condition a vital and natural creativity, free from affectation and constraint; and, according to the foregoing remarks, it follows that the computer functions in a completely different capacity, albeit an important one.

This capacity enables the composer to concentrate upon more creative concerns by obviating the purely technical preliminaries so characteristic of the analog electroacoustic studio set-up, eliminating details that normally encumber the compositional task, and allowing him to work more efficiently in an environment conducive to exploration and adventure.

Listeners crave arousal and radiance of beauty. They need to be inspired with courage and hope. Unfortunately, many composers active today in the world's most technologically sophisticated centers for digital electroacoustic music produce material evincing few of these essential attributes. This is indicative of the fact that the most advanced digital hardware and software cannot camouflage a composer's lack of talent and imagination. In other words, "You've either got it, or you don't!"

* * *

In addition to this obsessive behavior of composers, a central problem yet to be tackled is one in which computers are perceived as machines by noncomposers. It would be appropriate here to present two typical dialogues:

"What instrument do you play?"
"The computer."
"No, seriously, what do you play?"
"I play the computer."

With that final affirmation, the conversation comes to a grinding halt.

Occasionally, musicians who know I am involved in electroacoustic music will inquire:

"What instrument do you play?"
"The computer."
"No, seriously, what do you play?"
"I play the computer."

Experiencing a sense of frustration at what appears to be a futile situation, they persevere with:

"OK, Robin, you want to be manipulative? Then tell us what *regular* musical instrument do you play?"

I in turn ask with Talmudic flair:

"Why is the computer *not* a regular musical instrument?"

At this juncture they surrender and the dialogue ends.

To clarify my point, please indulge this allusion to technology. I should like to describe a mechanical apparatus with which I am

Compare
computer
to piano
movement

quite familiar and whose configuration is most labyrinthine. It consists of sundry interrelated parts with separate functions, and these are used in the performance of a special kind of work: (a) it has almost ninety switches, which, when pressed, trigger a corresponding number of devices not unlike hammers (both in appearance and function); (b) once these hammerlike contrivances have been activated, they come into contact with rigid bodies that are forced from a state of equilibrium and begin to fluctuate repeatedly above and below some mean value (as the pressure of a soundwave).

If you have not yet guessed, I am talking about a machine that possesses more moving parts than the computer—a device of such intimidating dimensions that today I only wish I had learned to play the trumpet as a child. Yes, I am talking about the piano.

In the 280 years that have elapsed since the Paduan Bartolomeo Cristofori (1655–1730) invented this instrument, people have grown accustomed to its face. The greatest opposition it suffered as a new instrument was due to the fact that people did not know how to play it and did not understand its virtues.[1] Similarly, the advent of computer music was met with awe and wonder, if not outright disquiet. Certainly, one would think that sufficient time has passed since the pioneering efforts of the late 1950s to allay this state of apprehension and psychic tension. But sadly, the past and present are striking for the computer music composer's indulgent disregard of this profound emotional effect his music has upon the listener.

The conduct of the composer in the digital media is excessively intellectual and oriented with a view to rendering the composition intelligible in as unintelligible a way as possible. The originator and developer of Gestalt Therapy, Frederick S. Perls, spoke of the intellect as "the whore of intelligence."[2] The implication here is that, with all the musical energy misdirected because of excessive intellectualization, the composer does not see or hear any more. Unfortunately, there is so much of this "pandering" in computer music today that many of our artistic sensibilities—the very capacity for acoustic discovery and for making discriminating aesthetic judgments—have been dulled in the process. As a consequence, one notes the cool indifference of the dissatisfied "customer" in the face of a music that does not take him into account.

What I am therefore recommending is a more humanistic, gestalt-motivated approach to the digital electroacoustic media. This would entail the creation of a new mode of thought characterized by compassion and tenderness for one's fellow-traveler on the musical journey—a new social dynamic in which all those who are involved are imbued with loving kindness and affection, are free from small-mindedness, free from having a prejudiced and morally self-righteous mind and petty resentfulness.

I am talking about a dynamic characterized by an exalted moral excellence and a thoughtful and sympathetic concern. Understandably, more than a mere scheme to be examined, the new computer music composition should be an act of generosity—an act of offering for acceptance. Without the composer's readiness to give, without his being painfully sensitive to the listener's pressing organismic needs, he must not expect the listener to ennoble his interests, values, and dignity. Similarly, the listener must also consider the composer's welfare and must do so with vigilance if he is to prove at all receptive to the composer's work.

What I am suggesting is not mawkish sentimentality but rather a new interactive context in which both composer and listener function as equal and active participants in a pivotal transaction. It is only with such mindfulness that communion and a refined, heightened musical sensitivity can be reached in these media, which is the very essence of postwar compositional development and which points the way to the twenty-first century.

Notes

1. Arthur Loesser, *Men, Women, and Pianos: A Social History,* (New York: Simon & Schuster, 1954), pp. 33–34.

2. Frederick S. Perls, *Gestalt Therapy Verbatim,* (New York: Bantam Books, 1981), p. 24.

Computer Music or Computer Music?

John Melby
UNIVERSITY OF ILLINOIS AT URBANA-CHAMPAIGN

Speaking at the Second Annual Music Computation Conference in 1975 at the University of Illinois, Hubert S. Howe, Jr., one of the pioneers in computer music, observed that "people are apparently much more interestd in new programs, facilities, and methods than they are in the music that is made possible by these procedures." He continued, "Surely this is backwards. It is like arguing that the importance of a body of music is in the technical principles it embodies rather than in its value as a musical experience. It might be alleged, for example, that the value of electronic music is in the development of the technical procedures by which it is put together, or that the value of the music of the seventeenth and eighteenth centuries was the development of the system of triadic tonality and the gradual adoption of tempered tuning. How can such abstract principles be more important than the music that embodies them?"[1]

How, indeed? And yet it is demonstrable that the annual computer music conferences that have been held almost every year since 1974 are almost entirely devoted to technical papers, and that when they are concerned with compositional matters, the topic is usually one that deals with some sort of algorithmic procedure for generating musical structures (I have been guilty of this myself) and not with the question of "composition," at least in the traditional sense of the word. (One could, of course, argue that the most important phrase in the preceding sentence is "in the traditional sense of the word," and that there is no reason for the word "composition" to be qualified thusly.)

It seems to me that during the past few years there has been a marked shift on the part of some composers away from the old idea of music's being written for an "audience," or at least away from a conception of the audience as the heterogeneous group of (for the most part) musically literate persons of varying backgrounds, toward the idea of an audience consisting mostly of colleagues with similar interests and education. This situation is not, of course, limited to composers of computer music. Indeed, as the means of musical expression have become more difficult for the layperson to follow, such a development has become almost inevitable. Nor is it entirely an unfortunate situation. After all, as Milton Babbitt has pointed out,[2] there is no reason to expect an uninformed listener to be able, at least when a given compositional technique is first introduced and utilized, to understand it any more than there is reason to expect a reader whose previous literary experience is confined to the novels of Jacqueline Susann to be able to make sense of *Finnegans Wake*. One hopes that the situation will improve over the years, but it must be kept in mind that a work of art will never, regardless of how good it is, be accessible to everyone.

However, along with this shift toward a more specialized audience, which may be salutary, there is a more insidious kind of change in the way in which composers sometimes view the audience for their music. This has to do not with the makeup of that audience but rather with the nature of that audience's response to the music: namely, that the audience is expected to respond not to the composition itself as an *objet d'art* but to view as its primary area of concern the process by which the work was produced. Thus, any idea which is in and of itself intriguing is regarded as suitable for the generation of a piece of music without consideration of whether or not the idea seems to be one that can yield fruitful results when applied to auditory phenomena.

Concomitant with this trend has been an increase in the number of "composers" who are either totally or largely untrained in their discipline. The reason for this is not difficult to trace; in art generally, the twentieth century can be regarded as the "age of the dilettante." With the relaxation of the rules by which certain numerous musical structures (chord formations, interval successions, etc.) were formerly regarded as *verboten,* and with the proliferation of different musical stylistic approaches, it has become relatively easy for anyone to become a composer simply by proclaiming himself/herself as one. Of course, there are many musicians who regard the wide-open situation referred to above as urgently emphasizing the need for a composer to impose restrictions upon himself/herself in order to bring order out of chaos, and I have no qualms about allying myself with this group. However, at least in some circles, these musicians are considered fusty old conservatives who are living in a bygone, more authoritarian age, and there is at least one group that regards those who advocate such an approach as fascists.

The emphasis on process mentioned above and the newly-found ability of anyone to proclaim himself a composer have combined to wreak havoc in electronic music. It is well known that at any period in music history, it is very difficult for contemporaries to make judgments of the worth and ultimate "staying power" of musical compositions. One need only look at the music of the nineteenth century to realize that many of the most highly regarded composers of that time are now largely forgotten, while some of our judgments today concerning the status of "masterpieces" do not reflect those of critics and musicians of that time. This aspect of music alone causes enough trouble to make life difficult for the composer. When this problem is combined with the difficulties inherent in the appreciation of compositions written in a new medium that introduces its own new perceptual problems, the determination of the relative value of musical works becomes so problematical that the addition of untrained "composers" to the compositional "work force" greatly increases the difficulty of making reasonable judgments—even for the musician and the informed layman, much less for the uninformed person.

In the past, this situation was not as unfortunate as it has come to be in recent years, since the production of a composition in a form in which it could be performed required at least some musical knowledge, such as a rather good acquaintance with notation, etc., which usually has as a concomitant at least some acquaintance with theoretical and compositional techniques. (I exempt from this, of course, certain kinds of graphic notation.) However, with the advent of electronic music, in which compositions usually do not exist in notated form but rather as audio tapes, it became possible to a much greater degree than previously for someone with a purely technical knowledge of electronic music studio procedures to produce a "composition" in this medium. Since nothing is easier in the studio for someone with such knowledge than to produce a "pretty" sound, and since such sounds can easily be strung together in succession, there began to appear a rash of electronic pieces that possessed some immediate impact by virtue of their existence as a succession of such sounds but did not possess the underlying structural complexity and formal coherence that provide a composition with lasting value.

The immediate feedback possible in the electronic medium thus provided the amateur, as well as the professional, the opportunity to "improvise" in the studio. I do not at this point mean to downgrade the usefulness of such improvisation; on the contrary, many composers have found such procedures highly useful in their creative work. However, the experienced composer generally uses such activities as a point of departure for a highly sophisticated shaping of the improvised material in order to produce a finished composition, whereas the amateur often leaves the improvised material to serve as the final product, which usually is lacking in overall structural coherence and interest, although it may possess a certain surface charm that suffices for one or two hearings.

Until recently, this type of immediate feedback, so useful but at the same time so dangerous, has not been generally available to the composer of computer music. However, with the introduction of the relatively inexpensive digital synthesizer, real-time systhesis is becoming a reality that threatens to produce a situation in computer music comparable to that outlined in the previous paragraph. This is, of course, not a valid reason for resisting such change, even if such resistance could have any effect, which it obviously cannot. The benefits for composers to be derived from immediate feedback far outweigh any problems that it may cause. However, I do think that it may be high time for some of the international computer music conferences that are held annually to include some discussions on exactly what the nature of computer music should be, or perhaps more realistically, what it is.

At the present time, I firmly believe that many of the sweeping statements that have been made in the recent past concerning the supposed "revolutionary" character of computer music have been somewhat overdone. To be sure, the possibility of producing music by means of digital computers has opened up many avenues for exploration that have not existed before. However, it seems to me that as things stand now, we are still dealing, as we have in the past, with a new *medium* and not with a fundamentally different *kind* of music. I believe that the primary considerations of the composer of computer music are not that different from those of the composer of music for many more traditional media, and that the computer is still useful primarily as a means of synthesizing electronic sound.

It is, of course, quite possible and even probable that this situation will change as artificial intelligence develops over the next few decades. Even now, many composers, including me, have made use of the algorithmic capabilities of the computer in the designing of the structural procedures underlying their works. Such use of the computer will doubtless continue to increase in the near future, as is only natural. However, the examples of "computer-composed music" that I have heard do not convince me that such music will have a significant role in music at large for many years to come. It seems to me that the primary virtue of using the computer for the purpose of making compositional decisions is that of *extending* the traditional human compositional processes rather than offering an alternative; and we know so little about those processes themselves that such extensions will take a great deal of time and experimentation.

One of the greatest problems with which the composer of music for digital computer must deal is a misunderstanding of the relationship of the medium to the compositional process on the part, unfortunately, of noncomposer colleagues rather than of the musically-interested public. Specifically, I refer to the presence of misconceptions concerning how the computer can and/or should be used. (Such misconceptions are also frequently found in composers.) The most frequently encountered of these misconceptions deals with the almost infinite sound palette of the computer and the opinion of some listeners that a composition that does not make use of the full range of possibilities of the medium (which, if one thinks about it, is manifestly impossible!) is somehow invalid as a piece of computer music. One of my compositions, a work for voice and computer-synthesized tape, was recently criticized on this basis in a technical journal, in which the reviewer was critical of the fact that I had limited myself to a very narrow range of tone-colors, many of which were very simple in construction and some of which approached sine waves in character (although in fact there were no actual sine waves). He had, of course, a perfect right to make a criticism on the basis of the sound selection if he felt that the piece was less effective than it could have been as a result of it. However, his criticism was based upon his belief that the resources of the computer were underutilized. As a matter of fact, the narrow range of the sound choices was deliberate on my part, since I began with a basic conception of the piece as a piece of (to use a traditional analogue) "chamber music." In my own composition students, I often find that they have not given sufficient thought to whether or not a projected computer piece is "chamber" or "orchestral" in conception and that this often leads to a certain ambiguous quality in the scoring.

3) A related type of criticism is often encountered, namely that only those pieces should be written for computer that cannot possibly be produced in any other way. Aside from the fact that most music produced with the computer would be disqualified on this basis (and those who make this criticism would probably agree with that state of affairs), if this were the case, the computer would be virtually the only medium in which that situation prevailed. Pre-twentieth- and even twentieth-century music often exists in several forms: orchestral pieces, for example, arranged for piano duet, songs arranged for various instrumental combinations, piano pieces that exist also in orchestral versions, etc.—the list goes on and on. Even many twentieth-century masterpieces frequently cited as unrealizable in any form other than the original were presented by Schoenberg's Society for Private Performances in all sorts of outlandish combinations, reportedly very effectively (it is true, of course, that this was due to necessity—the pieces either had to be heard that way or not at all—but the fact remains that they worked). Medium, and the suitability of that medium to the composition, are, it seems to me, the business of the composer and no one else. One can choose to like the work or not to like it, but the piece should be accepted on its own terms and not judged on the basis of some hypothetical piece that does not exist.

Criticisms of pieces on the above-cited grounds are often encountered from composers, but they are most often made by persons with some expertise in computer music but none in composition. It is very important for the continued development of computer music that highly-skilled technical experts continue to contribute their knowledge and assistance to the development of new software and hardware. It is equally important (perhaps even more important), however, for the realization to become widespread that musical composition is a skill that takes many years to learn and develop and that a distinction must be made between a skilled technician and a composer.

It seems to me that the strides made in recent years in the development of sound synthesis techniques, the breakthroughs in sound production made possible through analysis and resynthesis studies, the improvements in software, and the design and development of sophisticated new hardware have caused many observers and practitioners to lose sight of one very important thing: the aim of computer music is (or, at least, *should* be) the enhancement of the capability to produce significant works of music utilizing the digital computer as a medium. The production of sound per se is, of course, a part of the whole process, but it is a means to an end and not the end in itself. It is time for discussions of computer music to give as much time to musical as to technical aspects. Or, to put it another way, it is time to realize that the goal of the entire process is computer *music* rather than *computer* music.

Notes

1. Hubert S. Howe, Jr., "Computer Music and Technology," in *Proceedings of the Second Annual Music Computation Conference*, ed. James Beauchamp and John Melby (Urbana: University of Illinois, 1975) 2:31–36.

2. Milton Babbitt, "Who Cares if You Listen?" *High Fidelity Magazine* 8, no. 2 (1958): 38–40, reprinted in *The American Composer Speaks*, ed. Gilbert Chase (Baton Rouge: Louisiana State University Press, 1966) 234–44.

The Quest for "Musically Interesting" Structures in Computer Music

David Keane

QUEEN'S UNIVERSITY

It used to be a truism that in computer music the technology was vastly ahead of the art. That is, that the means for directing the computer's power to achieve musical objectives were rudimentary in comparison to the seemingly unlimited potential for generating any particular sonic possibility. What we lacked was an efficient, flexible method for communicating our wishes to the computer *and* a sufficiently precise idea of what we actually wanted. It could have been said:

> The technology is ahead.
> The . . . tech . . . nology . . . is . . . ahead.
> Thetechnologyisahead.

But the days *have* caught up, and the control possibilities and our understanding of the inner workings of sound have been greatly improved. There remains, however, a shared general dissatisfaction with the music that is being produced by computer (along with all other types of contemporary serious music, I am compelled to add). While the computer may not be responsible for this situation, it does not seem to have contributed any improvements. An understanding of the computer itself is essential if it is to be used as a means of musical composition—but that understanding cannot be substituted for the understanding of how musical structure interacts with the human mind. I do not believe that the computer can significantly affect that relationship; it can only more or less satisfactorily participate in such a relationship. The computer, used intelligently, however, can certainly be of great value in finding out more precisely what that relationship is.

There are two principal issues: (1) what we have attempted to do, and (2) what we have achieved in that attempt. The attempts seem to be clustered at the poles of the range of possible strategies; excessive attention to microstructure vs. excessive attention to macrostructure; devotion to largely stochastic processes at every level vs. devotion to ultrarational processes at every level. As my following remarks will indicate, I feel that there is an overattention to those poles, which detracts from more significant issues. The terms "microstructure" and "macrostructure" suggest that there are only two places to look. In 1966, Elliott Carter hailed the developing "new" direction in music, which focused on larger structural considerations. He pointed out that "harmony" and "other matters" had become "simply details in a larger kind of concern."[1] My view is that music is not an experience based on one or two, or twenty, isolated aspects but very much the product of every aspect. A change in any aspect of a piece of music has an impact at the most fundamental level of our experience of the totality. A casual regard for details does not promise a very successful piece of music. Extravagant attention to macrostructural, microstructural, stochastic, or ultrarational approaches, to my mind constitutes casual regard for details.

If I make my statements in this paper strongly, I am motivated not so much by the conviction of my own infallibility as much as by a desire to make my position clear as efficiently as possible. Moreover, I make my points unequivocally because cautiously made statements are often too vague to be tested. In the end it is better to be *found* to be wrong than to *seem* to be right.

In the course of my remarks I will frequently quote and paraphrase the views of composers, particularly of those speaking at the dawning of the computer era. Most composers of the present are so engaged in their dialogues with the computers that they have no opportunity to sit down and write their thoughts about aesthetics, or as some have confessed, they have not really been able to formulate such ideas for themselves as yet.[2] Although I take an opposite point of view to most of the statements that I cite, I want to indicate that I respect the intelligence of these people. If I had not such respect, there would have been little value in dealing with their remarks. I wish to make clear that I am taking issue with the remarks and not the authors personally. I have extracted brief remarks that seem to me to fairly represent the intent of the author, at least at the time of writing. I have done so to paint a picture of the philosophical environment in which music is made today. While I deal with only part of that environment, I feel that it is both a major and a dangerous part. My response is an attempt to place what I consider to be erroneous views in their proper perspective. I do not for a moment believe that a piece of music can be "wrong." A piece of music is only more or less meaningful for each person who listens to it. But I do believe that accounts by composers of their aims and methods can be unknowingly incomplete and inaccurate and that such incomplete and inaccurate information can quickly become the foundation of the work of those who would emulate the music of such composers.

Among the principle strategies that have been the apparent basis for recent computer music are nine that I wish to examine. Each of these is based on a specious argument, the speciousness overlooked because composers have rejected the aesthetic fundamentals of music along with the purely technical aspects of former styles.

Pitch

Serial or Cell Structures

Music theorists tend to analyze notation rather than music. Our harvest from the labor of their researches has been a seduction into addressing a note, and by association, groups of notes, as a *thing*. We have stacked these notes like blocks and given these collections names. And in all of this stacking and naming we have forgotten that a note is in fact an amalgam of extremely complex, simultaneous, and sequential forces. When a violinist plays two notes he will choose one note to be subordinate to the other. If he chooses the first to lead to a stronger second note, he will make a crescendo on the first and accent the second. In that crescendo he will move the bow a bit closer to the bridge and apply more pressure, thus eliciting increasing strength of the overtones over the duration of the first note. He will support this by making a slight rising portamento on the first note, which will also result in a subtle but complex shift in relative strengths of the partials owing to the resonance characteristics of the strings, the sound box, and the room. And we have dealt only with the first note— one that is only a small contributor to the vast hierarchy of complimentary and opposing, fully discernible forces that comprise even the simplest well-played melody. Much of this is intuitive on the part of the player and intuitively assumed on the part of the composer.

Electroacoustic musical experience has revealed the astonishing error of the old unit analysis. But we seem to be aware of this interesting and valuable news at one moment and continue to operate on the basis of the old notational analysis the next. Truly, old ways die hard! In our example, the violinist has made the second note the logical consequence of the first. The combination of note-level and sub-note-level has bonded the elements into a thoroughly cohesive whole. Yet the next time the same two notes appear, the microprogression will likely be constructed to create a very different but equally cohesive whole. The microstructure in a piece of computer music is potentially capable of magnificently supporting the thrust of musical ideas but, so far, the microstructure has tended to merely *be* the thrust for its own sake.

Emulation of "Natural Structures"

In the spring of 1912, the Parisian Futurists published the following in *La Liberté*:

> The composers of today who are modern devotees of the past only deserve our contempt, for they labour in vain, composing original works with worn-out means. . . . Hear then the aesthetic laws of Futurism. These laws consist, in fact, of nothing more than the division of the octave into fifty intervals. The idea is physical in origin and has been considered repeatedly.[3]

I cite this passage to point out that even the Futurists, anarchists of the most virulent sort, were tempted to use "naturism" to make a case for the structural bases of their art. Although Henri Pousseur has admitted that art can "never encompass the universe and its fundamental nature," he nevertheless feels that artists can interpret "the world's message . . . through ordering, clarifying, and establishing relationships." John Cage claims that the most fundamental aspects of nature can be incorporated into art by embracing chance. The chance operations of nature are both the model and the content for Cage's music.[4]

Since at least the time of Pythagoras, we have been making Procrustean beds for musical elements and creating rationales for musical structure based upon these "facts of nature." It would be more valuable to try to understand science on the basis of what we learn from art rather than the reverse. The findings of science are not facts about nature but inferences about how *we perceive*—our only actual measures are our senses. In art the stimulus (the work of art) is relatively controlled; in science the stimulus (the universe) behaves according to laws entirely independent of us and known to us only in terms of the channels we develop most highly in our experience of art.

We see relationships and patterns in the universe because the stimuli are all decoded (or seem to be decoded) by the same mechanism—the human mind. Structure in nature is not a manifestation of nature but of the human mind. Unless the structure caters to the behavior of the mind itself rather than the conjectured behavior of natural processes external to the mind, emulation of a "natural structure" as a rationale for art is patently folly.

The more speculative our view of nature is, the more we tend to rely on structures that appeal first to the human mind. The best example of this are the various creation myths imagined by man. We can see their echo in all of the best work of man. When Gottfried von Leibnitz developed a system of binary counting at the end of the seventeenth century, he derived his greatest pleasure in pointing out the economy of the requirement of merely two symbols. To demonstrate a kind of divinity of the system he claimed: "Omnibus ex nihil decendis sufficit unum" ("One suffices to derive everything from nothing").[5] The ultimate fascination for Leibnitz, and for us, is the illusion of making something from nothing. To establish a system and to be faithful to it is trivial—the man-made world is glutted with such operations. But the conversion of musical base metals into gold is the magic with which our musical heroes have dazzled us. In Bach, Beethoven, Brahms, Debussy, Schoenberg, it is not the system itself or the faithfulness with which they operate in the system that we admire—it is how ingeniously the most rudimentary elements are formed and reformed with ever increasing power. The system's function is merely that of a guide to help us to look in the right place for this ingenuity.

Demonstrations of Hardware or Software

We are sufficiently familiar with this manifestation of the developing resources that little need be said, beyond including it for the sake of thoroughness. The extremely transitory nature of demonstration-compositions is owed not only to the changing fashions of art but even more so to the overwhelming pace with which a wonderful new technological trick becomes passé.

(Psycho)Acoustical Notions

Computers have been in particular invaluable not only for testing psychoacoustical theories but have provided the rich experience that generates such theories. Such things as spatial effects and synthesis and digital processing of "real" sounds have been the primary nuclei upon which many computer pieces have been structured. But these are really special cases of the demonstration-composition, and much as with any powerful technique in that category, the technique should support the musical objective, not be it. Of course, a piece may well incorporate such techniques and be an entirely successful work. The point is that the structure of a successful piece generates processes that engage the human mind. Technical strategies either should be subservient or at least should not impede those processes.

Some composers have approached sound in all of its manifestations as though it were the objective in itself. Several years ago at the UNESCO-sponsored International Computer Music Workshop in Aarhus, Denmark, the chairman of the project, Barry Truax, said that the only thing that is important to him is sound:

> I want to create a language, a musical language based on sound and the way it behaves. Therefore, I must know everything about sound that there is to be known.[6]

Yet he would exclude from that study, aesthetics—how people respond to intentionally structured sounds. Among the same remarks, Truax confessed:

> I promised to myself . . . to leave musical aesthetics on the shelf for a while; it is a very complicated little monster and I couldn't cope with it, and I thought it might be better to leave it and come back to it later in life when other things got sorted out.[7]

There is no doubt that aesthetics is a "very complicated little monster," but leaving it "on the shelf" would seem to mean that aesthetics are an optional consideration. But that is a mistake. Aesthetics (human response) and the study of sound (human response) are merely different filters through which we look at the same process. Whether a composer is aware of it or not, every compositional decision that he makes is based on a provisional assumption about aesthetics.

Timbre Experiments

Timbre experiments are a specific instance of the two preceding strategies but deserve to be singled out owing to the amount of attention that timbre has had in computer music and the contentiousness of the issue. Many composers have sought to provide the myriad low-level detail that is characteristic of mechanically-generated sounds by utilizing various forms of rapid random control of the various parameters that comprise timbre. To this approach, J. K. Randall has responded:

> The often deplored uniformity, monotony, or outright nastiness of electronic timbres seems to me more properly analyzed as a failure of some existing electronic compositions adequately to structure and develop their timbral components as elements of the composition, rather than any inherent debility in current technology or any musical dullness "inherent" even in the balder electronic timbres. A composition which meets the threat of triviality with a barrage of irrelevancies is at least as feeble a composition as one which has been "lushed-up" and perhaps a feebler one, in that it explicitly presents so many things which—specifically by virtue of electronics—could have been musically developed.[8]

Theoretically I think that Randall is correct, but I am not persuaded by his alternatives. He describes "lushed-up" timbres as "extra-structurally pre-filled garbage cans" and provides as an alternative simple mathematical transformations mapped onto the spectral envelope. This alternative is in itself no less "extra-structurally pre-filled" than the "lushing-up." Exponentiating partials by a constant, for example, may produce an interesting effect but does not in itself provide any particular structural relevance.[9] Yet either approach could be the basis of overcoming the "threat of triviality" by identifying the larger level progressions and putting this microstructural baggage to work in support of those progressions. I think that the consideration of how much is far more relevant at any given moment in a piece than what kind.

Show off the jargon of computers

The Program Note *assist the audience*

Compositions that would seem to have been inspired by an idea for a particularly splendid sounding program note are not new. But the tendency to produce them has been enhanced by the jargon-saturated possibilities of computerese. In the manner of demonstration-compositions, these pass very quickly into oblivion.

New Art in Response to New Means

At the Aarhus Workshop, Jean-Claude Risset spoke about "new musical possibilities,"[10] and Guiseppe Englert proclaimed that "a new way of compositional thinking is being called for by the new medium, the computer."[11] There are even those who maintain that listeners must alter their responses to music to meet the challenge of the new resources. But before we get too excited, we must answer the question: Are there really new musical possibilities or do we simply have new means of addressing the same musical potentials we have always had? Indeed, we have seen dramatic changes over the centuries in instrumentation, style, and—particularly significantly for our evaluation—notation, but the fundamental structural principles of opposition and developing variation (as Schoenberg called it, although he failed to see its universality) are powerfully at work overtly and covertly in every type of music to which we have access (I include in this traditional South Indian music, Roman plain song, and today's "bubble-gum" music among others).

The changes to which we give so much attention are changes in fashion. Ferruccio Busoni has said, "Spirit and emotion retain their essence, in the art work as in man himself; we admire technical achievements, yet they are outstripped, or cloy the taste and are discarded."[12] Great works of art are great despite the technical innovations they embrace, not because of them. Certainly fashions and the developing musical means are intimately interrelated. The development of better and better means (sounding boards for strings, keyboards for organs, valves for horns, computers for frustrated refugees from the analog studio) have allowed us ever greater subtlety and nuance, but not, in itself, better music. The music that speaks most directly and powerfully to human emotions is the most primitive. Structure, and control over structure, appeal to the intellect and these are what we have developed to the point of simply displacing the primitive essence of music. Music is necessarily an amalgam of both the sensed and the understood. One of these may outweigh the other, but if one entirely displaces the other, music is debased: either in the direction of physical violence or alternatively, in the direction of executive worry beads.

We have lost our sense of balance because we have failed to differentiate between means and content, and our notion of what music is for has been getting steadily fuzzier. The question is not, How must man adapt to suit the new possibilities in art, but rather, How can the new means be harnessed to suit man?

Complexity for Its Own Sake (Or for Its Mystical Properties)

Joel Chadabe's piece, *Solo,* is generated by a system that is partially under his control and partly determined (or "in-determined") by the system itself. With regard to the system, he states that he is "fascinated by unpredictable processes because their very nature suggests complexity.[13] Although unpredictable processes and complexity abound in our daily lives to a far greater extent than most of us would wish, some composers seek these conditions as objectives. I suspect that they do so for the pleasure that can be derived when the occasional comprehensible, or even interesting, result happens along. I see a good deal in common between the mathematician described by Tobias Dantzig and many of today's composers:

> The mathematician may be compared to a designer of garments, who is utterly oblivious of the creatures whom his garment may fit. To be sure, his art originated in the necessity for clothing such creatures, but this was long ago; to this day a shape will occasionally appear which will fit into the garment as if the garment had been made for it. Then there is no end of surprise and delight.[14]

For example, Guido Baggiani writes the following after presenting fifteen pages about how his digital piece was made:

> Very little or nothing of the composing categories used in *Senza Voci* will appear directly recognizable. Our hope is that music acts on different levels of perception: from a primary manifest level identifiable by everybody, to an ultimate secret level, perhaps acting on an unconscious background only, but that we confusedly sense, however, as necessary to the consistency of musical thought.[15]

It is curious that Baggiani's fifteen pages are addressed to what he sees as the "secret level," while the manifest level, the one that all listeners must encounter first, is left to fend for itself.

Originality for Its Own Sake

Gottfried Michael Koenig has observed that the composer is, "whether he is aware of it or not, under the impression of a musical tradition which values a composer's originality more highly than his skill in using established patterns."[16] We do not have to look far for evidence of the truth of Koenig's observation. Perhaps the most obvious place to look would be Milton Babbitt's famous article, "Who Cares If You Listen?" In it he says that the public's shunning of music that is too original "is not only inevitable, but potentially advantageous for the composer and his music. . . . The composer would do well to consider means of realizing, consolidating, and extending the advantage."[17] Babbitt says that the composer can use this opportunity to "probe the very foundations of his art." I cannot help but think the same line of reasoning would suggest that if a lecturer's audience were to suddenly leave the room it would give him a golden opportunity to consider the ramifications of the alphabet.

What Babbitt advocates would seem to be masturbation. It is easy enough to guess what he gets out of "probing the very foundations of his art," but the residue of old orgasms has little interest for anyone else, now or *in* one hundred years. Yet there is something more than self-indulgence in Babbitt's position. Schoenberg thought that "the great artist must somehow be punished in his life-time for the honor he will enjoy later."[18] Ernst Krenek took the view that "the artist is immortal to the extent that he causes his contemporaries vexation."[19] Where views like these come from is easily surmised. We are sufficiently familiar with items like the following:

In 1881 John Ruskin wrote: "Beethoven sounds to me like the upsetting of bags of nails, with here and there an also dropped hammer."[20] In 1884, Charles Dancla wrote: "Brahms quartets for strings are meaningless, impossible and support no analysis."[21] Yet only twenty years later, Louis Elson wrote: "Poor Debussy, sandwiched between Brahms and Beethoven seemed weaker than usual. . . . There are moments when the suffering Faun in . . . *Afternoon of a Faun* seems to need a veterinary surgeon."[22] It comes then as no great surprise that a 1945 review in the *Pacific*

Coast Musician reads: "The Prelude to *Genesis* was by Arnold Schoenberg, the text for which was 'The Earth was without form, and void.' This reviewer has never heard music that had less form or was more nearly void than Mr. Schoenberg's contribution. It was simply a succession of ugly sounds bearing no relation whatsoever to the thing generally known as music."[23]

We know very well that comments like these have been hurled after nearly every composer whom we now regard as a master. What we forget is that the same kind of remarks were also directed at a vast multitude of *other* composers through the ages for whom the remarks were presumably perfectly applicable. In many of these cases, the negative comments do not seem to have proven any more worth preserving than the compositions to which they referred. This consideration not withstanding, we have seen during the second and third quarters of this century many misguided composers who would seem to have considered that incurring this kind of derisive reaction was both a necessary and sufficient condition for attainment of musical immortality.

The irony is that our preoccupation with derogatory comments seems to have overshadowed the fact that Beethoven, Brahms, Debussy, *and* Schoenberg were not really "ahead of their time." Had they been, neither their memory nor their music would have had any real possibility for being preserved or kept in the public eye. That great composers have had their detractors is no surprise—everything in our world seems to have its detractors; it is human nature. My point is that public antipathy is a nonissue; it is irrelevant. But Schoenberg would argue further:

> I believe that a real composer writes music for no other reasons than it pleases him. Those who compose because they want to please others, and have audiences in mind, are not real artists. . . . They are merely more or less skillful entertainers.[24]

We have already examined what pleases such composers, but I have selected this statement for its use of the word, "entertain." For some reason that word has come to have pejorative connotations in art and especially in music. If we examine the literal meaning of its Latin roots, *inter* and *tenere,* we see that the word means "to hold within." It seems to me that music is at its most effective moments when it *holds* its listeners *within* its own dimensions. The more listeners are able or wish to step outside the stream of events that comprise a piece of music, the less successful the work is.

It would seem to be true that many of our musical responses are subconscious. But that is no reason to *ignore* the conscious. The subconscious works most effectively in support of the conscious. If music fails to "hold" the conscious "within," there is no particular reason the subconscious will do any more than environmental monitoring. When music is primitively compelling, it forces its way into the conscious; when music is structured in a way that engages analytical and predictive processes, it invites itself into the conscious.

I would maintain that composers should use every level of every aspect of every possible means to engage and hold the listener's attention. Because the potential listener will not attend to every detail in no way implies that the composer should not. The less the music relies on established conventions, the greater the effort the composer should make to insure his language is accessible. Intuition relies on previous experience. To the degree that the music is outside of conventions, the composer must make a conscious effort to create structures that teach the new language, and he must know the language well enough himself so that he not only speaks it but speaks eloquently.

My concern is nicely summarized in the following paraphrase of an observation once made by A. S. Eddington:

> We have found strange sounds on the frontiers of the unknown. We have devised profound theories, one after the other, to account for the purpose of these sounds. But at last we have succeeded in reconstructing the creature for whom they were made.
> And lo, it is us.[25]

Bibliography

Babbitt, Milton. "Who Cares If You Listen?" *The American Composer Speaks*. Edited by G. Chase. Louisiana State University Press, 1966, pp. 234–43.

Baggiani, Guido. "*Senza Voci*: Between Analog and Digital Composition." *Computer Music Report*. Edited by M. Battier and B. Truax. Ottawa: Canadian Commission for UNESCO, 1981, pp. 47–62.

Busoni, Ferruccio. *The Essence of Music and Other Papers*. Translated by R. Ley. London: Rockliff Publishing Corporation, 1957.

———. "Sketch of a New Esthetic of Music." *Three Classics in the Aesthetic of Music*. New York: Dover Publications, 1962, pp. 73–102.

Cage, John. "Experimental Music." *The American Composer Speaks* Edited by G. Chase. Louisiana State University Press, 1966, pp. 226–33.

Carter, Elliott. "A Further Step." *The American Composer Speaks* Edited by G. Chase. Louisiana State University Press, 1966, pp. 145–54.

Chadabe, Joel. "*Solo:* A Specific Example of Realtime Performance," *Computer Music Report.* Edited by M. Battier and B. Truax. Ottawa: Canadian Commission for UNESCO, 1981, pp. 87–94.

Dantzig, Tobias. *Number: The Language of Science.* 4th ed. New York: The Free Press, 1967.

Englert, Guiseppe G. "Experiences Leading Towards Automated Composition." *Computer Music Report.* Edited by M. Battier and B. Truax. Ottawa: Canadian Commission for UNESCO, 1981, pp. 95–104.

Keane, David. "A Composer's View of Music Cognition, and Emotion." *Musical Quarterly,* 68, no. 3 (July 1982): 324–36.

———. "Architecture and Aesthetics: The Construction and Objectives of *Elektronikus Mozaïk*" in *Proceedings of the 1985 International Computer Music Conference.* San Francisco: The International Computer Music Association, 1985, pp. 199–206.

———. "At the Threshold of an Aesthetic," *The Language of Electroacoustic Music* (S. Emmerson, ed.). London: Macmillan, 1986, pp. 97–118.

———. "Computer Music: New Tools for Old Problems." *Humanities Association Review* 30, 1–2 (Winter–Spring 1979): pp. 103–113.

———. "Computer Music: Some Problems and Objectives in Applied Aesthetics." *Proceedings of the 1980 International Computer Music Conference.* 1980.

———. "Labyrinth: The Tangled Ways of Progression and Musicial Perception" in *Proceedings of the 13th International Congress on Acoustics.* Toronto: Canadian Acoustical Society, 1986, 3, K5–6.

———. *Tape Music Composition.* London: Oxford University Press, 1980.

Koenig, Gottfried Michael. "Composition Processes." *Computer Music Report.* Edited by M. Battier and B. Truax. Ottawa: Canadian Commission for UNESCO, 1981, pp. 105–26.

Krenek, Ernst. *Exploring Music.* Translated by M. Shenfield and G. Skelton. London: Calder and Boyars, 1966.

Randall, J. K. "Operations on Waveforms." *Perspectives on Contemporary Music Theory.* New York: W. W. Norton & Co., 1972, pp. 208–13.

Risset, Jean-Claude. "The Musical Development of Digital Sound Techniques." *Computer Music Report.* Edited by M. Battier and B. Truax. Ottawa: Canadian Commission for UNESCO, 1981, pp. 127–58.

Schoenberg, Arnold. *Style and Idea.* Edited by D. Newlin. New York: Philosophical Library, 1950–

Slonimsky, Nicolas. *Lexicon of Musical Invective.* 2d ed. Seattle: University of Washington Press, 1965.

Truax, Barry. "A Personal Assessment." *Computer Music Report.* Edited by M. Battier and B. Truax. Ottawa: Canadian Commission for UNESCO, 1981, pp. xxvii–xxx.

Notes

1. Elliott Carter, "A Further Step," *The American Composer Speaks,* G. Chase, ed. (Baton Rouge: Louisiana State University Press, 1966), p. 246–47.

2. Barry Truax, "A Personal Assessment," *Computer Music Report*, M. Battier and B. Truax, eds. (Ottawa: Canadian Commission for UNESCO, 1981), p. 173.

3. Ferruccio Busoni, *The Essence of Music and Other Papers*, R. Ley, trans. (London: Rockliff Publishing Corporation, 1957), p. 28.

4. John Cage, "Experimental Music," *The American Composer Speaks*, G. Chase, ed. (Baton Rouge: Louisiana State University Press, 1966), p. 230–31.

5. Tobias Dantzig, *Number: The Language of Science*, 4th ed. (New York: The Free Press, 1967), p. 15.

6. Truax, "A Personal Assessment," p. 172.

7. Truax, "A Personal Assessment," p. 173.

8. J. K. Randall, "Operations on Waveforms," *Perspectives on Contemporary Music Theory* (New York: W. W. Norton & Co., 1972), pp. 209–10.

9. Randall, "Operations on Waveforms," p. 210–13.

10. Jean-Claude Risset, "The Musical Development of Digital Sound Techniques," *Computer Music Report*, M. Battier and B. Truax, eds. (Ottawa: Canadian Commission for UNESCO, 1981), p. 130.

11. Guiseppe G. Englert, "Experience Leading Towards Automated Composition," *Computer Music Report*, M. Battier and B. Truax, eds. (Ottawa: Canadian Commission for UNESCO, 1981), p. 98.

12. Ferruccio Busoni, "Sketch of a New Esthetic of Music," in *Three Classics in the Aesthetic of Music* (New York: Dover Publications, 1962), p. 75.

13. Joel Chadabe, "*Solo:* A Specific Example of Realtime Performance," *Computer Music Report*, M. Battier and B. Truax, eds. (Ottawa: Canadian Commission for UNESCO, 1981), p. 88.

14. Dantzig, *Number,* p. 231–32.

15. Guido Baggiani, "*Senza Voci:* Between Analog and Digital Composition," *Computer Music Report*, M. Battier and B. Truax, eds. (Ottawa: Canadian Commission for UNESCO, 1981), p. 55.

16. Gottfried Michael Koenig, "Composition Processes," *Computer Music Report*, M. Battier and B. Truax, eds. (Ottawa: Canadian Commission for UNESCO, 1981), p. 109.

17. Milton Babbitt, "Who Cares if You Listen?" *The American Composer Speaks*, G. Chase, ed. (Baton Rouge: Louisiana State University Press, 1966), p. 236.

18. Arnold Schoenberg, *Style and Idea*, D. Newlin, ed. (New York: Philosophical Library, 1950), p. 24.

19. Ernst Krenek, *Exploring Music*, M. Schenfield and G. Skelton, trans. (London: Calder and Boyars, 1966), p. 243.

20. Nicolas Slonimsky, *Lexicon of Musical Invective*, 2d ed. (Seattle: University of Washington Press, 1965), p. 52.

21. Slonimsky, *Musical Invective*, p. 72.

22. Slonimsky, *Musical Invective*, p. 93.

23. Slonimsky, *Musical Invective*, p. 315.

24. Schoenberg, *Style and Idea*, p. 24.

25. Dantzig, *Number,* p. 230.

Aesthetic Appeal in Computer Music

Thomas E. Janzen

Introduction

People and machines neither hear nor make the same music. Machines measure and generate exact amplitudes, frequencies, time durations, and spectra. However, people hear and create music with subjective qualities such as rhythmic pulses, prettiness, illusions of the ear, imitations of sounds, models of nonmusical reality, freely rendered mathematical relationships, familiarity, archetypal symbols, and the stimulation of senses other than the auditory. We agree with Minsky's remark, ". . . Music should make more sense once seen through listeners' minds."[1] A reconciliation between machine and human purposes seems in order, to assure the promise of growing intimacy between machines and people. It is insufficient that a computer-music composer should think only in terms of the mean rate of vibrato of the oboelike sound in the next six seconds, without addressing the basic appeals of music. Leon Kirchner wrote; "One of the naive assumptions, in the construction of computer music, for instance, is that if one programs the parameters (duration, pitch, etc., etc.), music should result."[2] It is insufficient for composition and synthesis software to permit specification of only the notes and not of the musical impression to be made on the listener.

It is difficult to coax that irresistible object, music, from the immovable force that technically rather than humanly programmed computers represent. Nevertheless, composers persevere in an effort to program computers to make music the way they do. Laurie Spiegel reports on using the Groove program by Max Matthews and F. R. Moore: ". . . I wrote complex algorithms (in Fortran) to process the date from these devices (keyboard, knobs, pad, etc.) and derive from it much more complex music than I actually played . . . incorporating a set of rules for melodic evolution."[3] Writing about his composition program PHRASE, Hiller writes, ". . . the concept of hierarchy was little used in the early development of computer music algorithms. Because of this lack, I set about writing the programs . . ."[4] Clarence Barlow has said, "I found it necessary to work with computers because I began to write complex structurally organized pieces in the early 1970s."[5]

One high-level musical command can translate through several layers of problem-modeling to a single basic machine operation (e.g., add two quantities or move a piece of data). Such instructions are often necessary. However, as in APL or Lisp, some single high-level language instructions can also spawn a very complex series of machine events. Such instructions would be needed in a composition system that permitted general and human-oriented specifications for a work of music. Whether such software takes the form of a decision tree, as in program generators, or a compiler (perhaps occasionally asking assistance of the composer), or some other construct is left to implementors. It is likely that large numbers of personally customized default values and carefully randomized parameters will play an important role in such software.

Some suggested categories of musical appeal that composition software should address are discussed later. Music can interest a listener's personality in various ways and often not in ways that are intrinsically "musical." Music makes appeals to the whole personality. Excluded from the list of categories of appeal are those which do not depend only on musical sound, such as theatrical, visual, and literary elements.

The degree to which these sources of appeal inform a work of music is the measure of the listener's involvement, enjoyment, and enrichment. If the composition software impedes rather than assists the composer's endeavor to address these appeals, the result may be obscure and uncommunicative. All these appeals need not be thoroughly represented in a single work of music. It is more likely that the artistic personality of a composer will determine the relative strengths of the various elements.

The categories presented in this paper are kinesthetic stimuli, euphony, illusions of the ear, literal congruences, formal congruences, mathematics, convention, aural symbols, and synesthesia. The position in the list of any of these categories can be challenged, and the proposal of additional categories is welcome. This list is not exhaustive, and other categories undoubtedly exist.

Senses — Kinesthetic Stimuli

Involuntary reactions to rhythm and beat are experienced by every listener. The impulse to move or dance when one hears strong, pulsing music is a common experience. In the realm of new music, Stephen Wischerth's drum arrangements for Glenn Branca's Symphony no. 3 certainly exploit a profound kinesthetic and even tactile sensation in response to loud regular pulses.[6] The tactile sensation produced in the viscera by a large drum can be a powerful effect. Irregular rhythms have their own nervous effect. The combination of a regular pulse and a changing group of pulses appears in Steve Reich's *Four Organs* and in many imitative works in the idiom of digital synthesis.[7] In Reich's work, the constant pulse of maracas, stimulating a regular response, underlies organ chords that change duration and attack times. The effect is sometimes syncopated, becoming pleasantly disorienting as the chords lengthen. Subtle, less accented rhythms have a milder effect.[8] It is possible to quantify and control the degree of metric inevitability and regularity, as Barlow has done in such works as *Çoğluoautobüsişletmesi*.[9] Rhythm, then, becomes a kinesthetic stimulus as well as an organizing tool.

Euphony

The appeal of euphonious sounds depends in part on historical trends of taste. Today many chords now thought pretty were, a hundred years ago, regarded as piercing dissonances awaiting resolution. Whatever values prevail at the moment, music often depends on being pleasant to the ear. Computer sound synthesis has made use of especially consonant chords, by tuning the tones to just (integer ratio) intervals. Consonance has even been quantified. An interval is consonant when it is a unison or close to it, or more than a critical bandwidth apart, and dissonant at one-quarter critical bandwidth (about 600 Hz, a twentieth of an octave).[10] Modern electronic instruments have revived an interest in just and other consonant intonations, as heard in some of Laurie Spiegel's works.[11]

Certain instrumental colors can be thought of as euphonious. The sounds of a Theremin, a pure sine tone, chimes, glass harmonica, celestas, and glockenspiels come to mind. Although listeners may tire of these sounds in several seconds, the instruments make an appeal to a sense of prettiness.

A computer music work need not make this appeal to prettiness, and in fact may fight such an appeal in order to argue an idea incompatible with euphony. *HPSCHD*, by John Cage and Lejaren Hiller, although a persuasive work, is not a pretty piece.[12] Hiller's large number of simultaneous electronic tapes for *HPSCHD* comprise a wonderful noise, to be sure, but not a consonant, pretty sound to charm the ear. Iannis Xenakis's intense computer-generated sound work *Mycenae-alpha* also comes to mind.[13] Euphony is a resource and a changing value, to be seduced or battled.

Illusions of the Ear

Composers and performers exploit the ear's mistakes in perception.[14] Oboes change tone-color to suggest a change in dynamics of which the instrument is incapable. *Shephard's Tones* by R. N. Shephard fools the ear with constantly ascending scales, seemingly forever without turning back.[15] As the scale ascends, its higher harmonics are attenuated, obscuring the actual octave placement of the fundamental. The effect of "shifting down the spectral distribution while all components go up" is exploited by Jean-Claude Risset in his *Mutations*.[16] These and other illusions must be taken into account in the effect of music, since unintentional illusions may go unrecognized, possibly harming the composer's intent. Music binaurally recorded or synthesized for earphone audition is especially well-adapted to exploit sound-location illusions and pitch-motion illusions.[17] Composition and synthesis software should catalog illusions and make them available, as well as flag unintentional illusions in a score. The exact control provided by computer synthesis may permit specification of illusions, especially in works meant for earphone audition.[18]

mimics — **Literal Congruences**

Literal congruences with the perceptual world are simply imitations of sounds in the world. They include onomatopoeia and the imitation of bird calls in Olivier Messiaen's music. The voice is its own imitator, and computerized voice synthesis may also represent a literal congruence with the human voice, as in *Speech Songs* by Charles Dodge.[19] Imitating traditional musical instruments represents the use of literal congruence and is a major preoccupation of computer composers such as Jean-Claude Risset.[20] Tape music employing recorded sounds from the wider world depends on the same appeal that photographs do: the recognition of something familiar in the artist's creation, in a more or less obscure presentation. Digital recording and processing of sound opens up new expressive possibilities. The effective modulation of the obscurity of the sound image can tease the listener's attention and make the sound more compelling. The resynthesis of Enrico Caruso's voice in Charles Dodge's *Any Resemblance Is Purely Coincidental* exploits this effect.[21] With digital sampling instruments, knob and keyboard inputs permit the reproduction and manipulation of natural sounds in the context of computer music. This has led to a rich new tradition, following earlier ground-breaking work in musique concrète with magnetic tape.

Formal Congruences

Formal congruences occur in music when abstract relationships in sound resemble such relationships in the world. Whereas literal congruences mimic the world's surface, formal congruences mirror its structure. This "world" can be cognitive or perceptual or both. Formal congruence is commonly expressed in musical structure. Musical events can occur in sequence in semblance to some sequence of events observed elsewhere. Recognized patterns with which music imitates life include repetition, growth, and adversary relationships. When solo concerti are expositions of the principle of the individual prominent in a crowd, or against a crowd, a formal congruence is in use. Manfred Clynes believes he has found direct correspondences between the inflection of well-formed melodies and the energy contour of ordinary spontaneous emotional responses.[22] A composition process that employs mathematics can also create a formal congruence, such as a Gaussian distribution of speed in a section of music similar to a distribution of a gas, in *Pithoprakta*.[23] Software for automatic composition should permit (and has permitted in many instances) the composer's description of overall shapes and relationships in music, assigning the task of choosing specific quantities and events to the program itself.

Mathematics

The traditional contrapuntal manipulations of a motif represent a permutational logic. It flourished in this country as serialism, but these manipulations have their origins in the beginnings of literate music. The symbols of linguistic syntax and transformational grammar also have been used by composers, notably in computer composition.[24] The stochastic music of Iannis Xenakis is well known. It is built with models from statistical mathematics.[25] By using mathematical models and methods to generate structure and sound, "it is therefore conceivable that a single self-similar stochastic process could generate both the overall structure and the sound texture of a piece".[26] Many composers, including Bartók, Cage, Debussy, and Bach, have used the ratio of the golden mean as a means of partitioning musical time. The affinity of the composer's mind for mathematical thought is not surprising. Music and mathematics are both concerned primarily with self-referential relationships, and both require a penchant for formal detail.

The acuity with which the listener apprehends a mathematical schema depends on the structural level at which the schema is applied, and it is not necessary that the mathematical organization be decipherable in order to play a role in the music's expression. Correctly analyzing by ear alone the microscopic path of the pitch-class set in Webern's *Variationen für Klavier* would speak to a great gift.[27] But most listeners could be expected to hear a difference if that profoundly poetic work were rewritten with the same serial organization but a different pitch-class set. However, large scale mathematical organization of sound, such as in some works of Xenakis, can be subjectively clear to listeners, especially if suggested in advance in the composer's program notes. The use of computers in composition permits more pervasive and complex mathematical models to inform works of music, and composition software should enhance these possibilities.

Convention

Convention is a framework of familiarity. The listener is drawn into a work with a familiar sound or rhetoric. Parodies (imitations) of historical idioms (for example, Bach's counterpoint or expressionistic serialism) employ convention's appeal. Even using a familiar contemporary idiom invokes the appeal of familiarity. Expectations based on previous listening experience are cajoled into surprise or disappointment from the established context. Poly-idiomaticism juxtaposes idioms and produces an eclectic vocabulary.

Although no music is without precedent, a composer can, intentionally violate a prevailing tradition so violently that the music seems to the listener to bear no relation to what is expected from music. In *Shibucho,* Carl Stone uses a digital delay and harmonizer to process (in real-time on stage) the output of a phonograph playing "vernacular music."[28] The inputs were ordinary popular tunes, but the output derived from them is a completely unpredictable cubist reassembly pursuing less mundane musical values.

Convention is often difficult to escape. The convention of the equal-tempered scale still weighs heavily on composers' shoulders today, precisely because there is such a vast installed base of tonal instruments that have been built particularly to reproduce approximations of that scale. It may be the single greatest influence on iterative euphony, such as that of Philip Glass and Steve Reich. Grand pianos, the Boehm-fingered wind instruments, and valve brass instruments, although imperfect, are built, and their instrumentalists are taught to strive for equal-tempered intonation. In the pursuit of performances, composers generally use this scale rather than experiment with other sounds because it is so convenient to do so. The availability of digital sound synthesis and acoustic-source sound processing has made it convenient to experiment with various scales as well as with sounds without definite pitch. This has immeasurably broadened the literature and tradition.

Quotations reincarnate popular tradition in the works of Charles Ives, notably the First Sonata.[29] Quotations can also become a symbol and proclaim the composers' relation to tradition, as in the movement "The Abyss of Time" in Crumb's *Makrokosmos I,* which refers to Chopin's Fantasie-Impromptu in C-sharp minor.[30] Paul Lansky has described a musique concrète treatment of traditional music in his *Folk Images.*[31]

Convention, then, becomes a tool, like a musical instrument, that a composer calls into use when needed and employs for special expressive purpose. Composition software should facilitate the inclusion of music in the public domain.

Aural Symbols

Perhaps aural symbols appeal to psychic archetypes. Carl Jung provided a vocabulary for therapeutic visual art and myth.[32] More research in musical symbols is needed. We can guess at some possibilities. Symbolic musical appeals may appear in sounds resembling: buzzing bees, the squealing of pigs, an infant's wail, a hound's howl, cries[33], barks, squeals (anima symbols?), breaking glass (perhaps the shock of some sounds may provoke reflexes in a kinesthetic response, but also stimulate the inner psyche), and the harmonic series (a mandala symbol?). It seems likely that certain fundamental musical constructs may have some archetypal appeal. The falling melody, the stepwise melody, and the centric melody found in world music may perhaps make such appeals.[34] Again, Clynes may have a key to the expression in melodic shapes.[35] Other symbolic appeals are not directly musical. These include the apparent use of numerology by J. S. Bach, George Crumb, and others, and symbolic notation, especially of Crumb. The movements "Crucifixus," "The Magic Circle of Infinity," and "Spiral Galaxy" from *Makrokosmos I* are all "drawn" rather than written in the shape of a cross, a circle, and a spiral, respectively.[36] Graphical score editing software such as Xenakis's UPIC system allows the score to be "drawn" in a variety of forms, which could include archetypal symbols.

Synesthesia

When listeners allow music to suggest sensations from sense organs other than the ear, they enjoy a synesthetic sensation. What color is a chord, or how does a dissonance feel? True synesthetes are involuntary.[37] The hallucination of colors in response to sound is called chromesthesia. Is this a basic appeal that a composer can exploit? We know that Messiaen personally associated particular colors with particular chords, and his melodic modes; and the linkage of color and sound in Scriabin's music is well known. Do multimedia artists, such as Laurie Anderson, intend a synesthetic connection between the music, the film, and the stage movement?[38] It seems unlikely: synesthesia is inherently redundant; the different senses feel the same stimulus. Multimedia works usually seem to create complementary statements in the difference media, so that Anderson's films and her postliterate electronic collage converse with, not mimic, one another.

A suggestion of intent is always possible in titles and program notes, for the suggestible and uninhibited listener.

Conclusion

I have set forth nine categories of appeal in computer music. Listeners often do not clearly hear and apprehend exact frequencies, amplitudes, and durations. Listeners can perceive qualities such as prettiness, familiar relationships, or a provocation to the musculature. The categories offered in this paper need not—and indeed should not—always be in equal balance in an expressive artist's work. However, ignoring such responses may inhibit expression.

Intellectual challenge and the carrying of ideas are basic to western music. Music's concern is its ideas, which must be expressed in means that listeners hear. The question for the composer is always, "What will be heard when my piece is played?" not "What is the mean frequency of the oboe vibrato in the next six seconds?" Listeners rarely notice the latter, but the former is the meaning in the music.

Notes

1. M. Minsky, "Music, Mind and Meaning," *Computer Music Journal* 5, no. 3 (1981): 28–44.

2. P. Ramey, liner notes for Columbia MS7284. String Quartets by Kirchner and Weinberg.

3. L. Spiegel, *The Expanding Universe.* Philo Records 9003 (1980).

4. L. Hiller, "Composing with Computer: A Progress Report," *Computer Music Journal* 5, no. 4 (1981): 7–21.

5. S. Kaske, "A Conversation with Clarence Barlow," *Computer Music Journal* 9, no. 1 (1985): 19–28.

6. G. Branca, *Symphony No. 3 (Gloria) Music for the First 127 Tones of the Harmonic Series* (New York: Neutral N-4, 1983).

7. S. Reich, *Four Organs* (Hollywood: Angel S-36059, 1970).

8. G. Cooper and L. B. Meyer, *The Rhythmic Structure of Music* (Chicago: University of Chicago, 1960).

9. S. Kaske, Ibid.

10. M. V. Mathews, *The Technology of Computer Music* (Cambridge: MIT Press, 1969).

11. L. Spiegel, Ibid.

12. J. Cage and L. Hiller, *HPSCHD for Harpsichords and Computer-generated Sound Tapes* (New York: Nonesuch H-71224).

13. I. Xenakis, *Formalized Music* (Bloomington: Indiana University Press, 1971).

14. B. Patterson, "Musical Dynamics," *Scientific American* 231, no. 11 (1974): 78–95. D. Deutsch, "Musical Illusions," *Scientific American* 233, no. 10 (1975): 92–98 and 103–4.

15. R. N. Shephard, *Shephard's Tones* (New York: Decca DL710180).

16. J.-C. Risset, "Computer Music Experiments 1964," *Computer Music Journal* 9, no. 1 (1985): 11–18. Also Risset's "Digital Techniques and Sound Structure in Music," in C. Roads, ed., *Composers and the Computer* (Los Altos: Kaufman, 1985), pp. 113–138.

17. M. R. Rosenzweig, "Auditory Localization," *Scientific American* 205, no. 4 (1961): 132–142.

18. G. Kendall and W. Martens, "Simulating the Cues of Spatial Hearing in Natural Environments," in W. Buxton, ed., *Proceedings of the 1984 International Computer Music Conference* (San Fransisco: Computer Music Association, 1984), pp. 111–126.

19. C. Dodge, *10 + 2: 12 American Text Sound Pieces* (Berkeley: 1750 Arch Records, 1973).

20. J.-C. Risset, Ibid.

21. C. Dodge, *Any Resemblance is Purely Coincidental. Computer Music Journal* 7, no. 1 (1983): excerpt on a sound sheet. Also New York: Folkways Records FSS 37475.

22. M. Clynes, "Music Beyond the Score," *Magazine-Journal of the Bodily Arts and Sciences* 5, no. 1 (1985): 4–14.

23. I. Xenakis, Ibid.

24. S. R. Holtzman, "Using Generative Grammars for Music Composition," *Computer Music Journal* 5, no. 1 (1981): 51–64.

25. I. Xenakis, Ibid.

25. T. Bolognesi, "Automatic Composition: Experiments with Self-Similar Music," *Computer Music Journal* 7, no. 1 (1983): 25–36.

27. A. Webern, *Variationen für Klavier*, Op. 27 (New York: Universal Edition, 1937).

28. C. Stone, "New Music America: Biographies of Festival Participants." Notes on *Shibucho* in *High Performance* 8, no. 3 (1985): 50–68.

29. C. E. Ives, *First Sonata* (New York: Peer, 1910).

30. G. Crumb, *Makrokosmos Volume 1 for Amplified Piano* (New York: C. F. Peters, 1974).

31. C. Roads, "Interview with Paul Lansky," *Computer Music Journal* 7, no. 3 (1983): 16–24.

32. C. G. Jung, *The Spirit in Man, Art and Literature*. Translated by R. F. C. Hull (Princeton: Princeton University Press, 1966).

33. L. Anderson, "Sharkey's Day" on *Mister Heartbreak* (Burbank: Warner Bros., 1984).

34. C. Sachs, *The Wellsprings of Music* (New York: McGraw-Hill, 1965).

35. M. Clynes, Ibid.

36. G. Crumb, Ibid.

37. B. Lemley, "Synethesia: Seeing is Feeling," *Psychology Today* 18, no. 6 (1984): 65.

38. L. Anderson, *United States* (New York: Harper & Row, 1984). *United States* (Burbank: Warner Bros. 25192-4, 1984).

Part 3
Individual Systems:
The Development of Personal Styles

Electronic Sonata

Lejaren Hiller

STATE UNIVERSITY OF NEW YORK AT BUFFALO

Electronic Sonata is a composition I completed in 1976, which had a quite colorful, if not downright peculiar genesis. For this reason I thought it might be interesting to recount some of this history, because I rather think this history says something about how musical compositions come into existence and how composers work in the real world. Often I think this has little to do with analytical schemes that appeal to analysts or with aesthetics, which too often is a means of making an art product a marketable commodity. Both serve a useful end, here as in all music—an expressive one. It helps of course to know how a piece is assembled into a particular structure, and of course it also helps if a composer has some notion as to why he makes the artistic decisions he makes, and I shall indulge in some of this presently. I shall even discuss some of the technical aspects of its creation, but it should be well understood that these are merely means to an end. Let me start by describing the piece itself.

Electronic Sonata is a fifty-three minute work for tape alone. The preferred format is four channels, but naturally, it often gets played in two-channel reduction for purely practical reasons. It is a single-movement work in sonata form—but in a sonata form that is different from the usual in its dialectic. Here the contrast is not between tonic and dominant in the exposition versus a re-emphasis of the tonic in the recapitulation; it is instead a contrast of sounds generated by means of a computer as main subject versus concrète sounds as second subject. Moreover, the second subject of the exposition is derived largely from the sounds of nature (wind and waves, thunder, insects, etc.), whereas the second subject of the recapitulation is concerned primarily with man-made sounds, i.e., machinery in a multitude of its forms.

123

The principal computer-generated sound complexes are of two types. The first are endlessly repeating glissandi that realize Drobisch's helical concept of tonality proposed in 1846 and greatly expanded upon and made programmable much more recently at Bell Telephone Laboratories by R. N. Shepard and J.-C. Risset. Drobisch's concept is shown in figure 1. Note that in this diagram, pitch level is measured vertically and that notes of the scale within each octave are measures around the circumference of a circle. In many ways, these glissandi also resemble "impossible objects" as drawn by M. C. Escher.

In *Electronic Sonata,* I have used not only stable glissandi but also ones that accelerate and decelerate and are based upon many intervals narrower than the octave, even down to microtones. Included among these is the interval of the golden mean (1.612), derived from the Fibonacci series, which played such an important role in classic architecture. The reason for its inclusion involves the history of the piece, which I shall deal with presently. Anyway, all these glissandi were produced with the State University of New York computer music system that was in operation in 1975. This older system has since been replaced entirely, but briefly, it consisted of the following:

(1) A MUSIC 5 type program, which we adapted to our large CYBER computer in the University Computer Center, used by the entire university community. This program, refined over a period of some years, largely by R. F. Brainerd, carried out all the calculations expected from MUSIC 5 as written originally at Bell Laboratories by Max Mathews and his colleagues and wrote digital tape files counting the acoustical information normally at any rate up to 40kHz.

(2) These digital tapes were then carried to our electronic music studio, where we had a PDP-8 computer equipped with both a digital-to-analog converter and an analog-to-digitial converter. As anyone familiar with computer sound processing knows, this permits the conversion of digital data into electronic sound and vice versa. At that time, the vice versa was more of a novelty than now, and I exploited it for the second type of computer sound (see below).

Let us return now to the glissandi. In figure 2, I show how many glissandi set an octave apart can occur simultaneously. Here, frequency is plotted against time. It is possible to have glissandi move at a steady rate as shown here or to speed up or slow down. This is shown in figure 3, where frequency is plotted against what is essentially a time index.

Here the accelerating function represented by the curved line depicts a glissando moving twice as fast when it reaches the top of its range compared to when it starts. It is also possible to have any conceivable interval between simultaneous glissandi, as already noted above. These can be computed from a graph such as that shown in figure 4. All this can become quite technical and is in fact discussed in detail in a full report I have prepared that constitutes the "score" of this composition. The important point I wish to make here is rather that a rational process such as this can be developed to produce expressive and interesting sounds just as much as traditional musical resources.

The second type of computer sounds encountered in *Electronic Sonata* are metamorphoses of various sounds (electronic, concrète, vocal, and instrumental) that were introduced into the computer via analog-to-digital conversion. In the computer, two such sounds were mixed, not as in ordinary mixing but by interleaving the two lists of digits that represented the two sounds. This was done in such a way that one sound was gradually transformed into the other. The result was then returned to audio tape by digital-to-analog conversion. To the best of my knowledge, this still remains a novel process for sound transformation.

The concrète sounds that play a predominant role in *Electronic Sonata* were taken from a large variety of sources and are used unmodified in the exposition and recapitulation. Metamorphoses of these sounds as produced by the method just discussed occur principally in the development, analogous to the use of theme transformation in instrumental sonatas.

Let me now make a few brief remarks regarding the structure of the piece. I find whenever I compose music of any sort, there comes a point at which I like to fix a clear-cut structure for a piece, usually long before all the details are fully worked out. In other words, there comes a point where I focus attention on large-scale form (this may be quite aleatoric, by the way, if circumstances so dictate), and from there on I begin to fill in the details. Other composers may work differently, but this just happens to be my style. Another way to put it is that from here on I work deductively, going from the general to the particular. So I devise structures such as the one shown in figure 5 for the exposition. Similar schemes exist for the rest of the composition. It seems to me a layout like this is quite easy to follow in performance, and I would say that my experience in presenting this piece in public on numerous occasions reinforces this opinion.

I should now note that *Electronic Sonata* is actually also the central or "core composition" of a much larger work called *Midnight Carnival,* which is of indefinite duration and composed of many tapes besides this one. *Midnight Carnival* is intended to be performed in an urban environment with as many subsidiary events as can be collected together. Here we get into the history I spoke of earlier. *Midnight Carnival* was commissioned for the United States Bicentennial Celebration and was performed in St. Louis on 3 and 4 July in the whole downtown area of St. Louis, about twenty blocks in all. Approximately fifty thousand people came to the event, quite a difference from the usual scattering of people attending a typical avant-garde concert. In addition to the forty-six channels of sound I used to cascade all the electronic music up and down the streets, we had other electronic music, laser beam shows, and flatbed trucks with entertainments of various sorts. Thus, one might call *Electronic Sonata* the indoor, concert hall version of a musical concept and *Midnight Carnival* the outdoor, environmental realization of the same idea and much magnified at that.

The history of *Electronic Sonata* (and *Midnight Carnival*) actually goes back before the Bicentennial commission, and I rather think some of this is to the point. I believe it all started when the music director of a newly-formed Hollywood movie company called me one day late in 1974 to ask whether I would make some computer-generated "sound transformations" for a full-length animated film based on Ovid's *Metamorphoses*. I said maybe, because I had serious reservations about the quality of what we could accomplish with our limited equipment. Among other things, he wished quadraphonic sound, something we lacked at the time. Nonetheless, he and a company lawyer came East, and after the usual amount of haggling over terms (financial, technical, story content and so on), we struck a bargain.

With some of the money they advanced us, I finally could buy an up-to-date digital tape drive, which really put the system described earlier into business. The music director wanted glissandi and sound transformations but was vague as to detail, but I worked on it steadily and gradually began to formulate some of the sounds already described. So, in fact, the origin of this music was a proposed soundtrack for a movie of the style of *Fantasia* but on a famous classical topic. It was this context that led me to things such as the golden mean, and in fact, the descending glissando on the golden mean, now in the coda of *Electronic Sonata,* was originally intended to represent a descent into Hades. I might mention that the movie director had ideas of hiring famous pop singers such as Elton John to sing songs that some of this material was meant to accompany, farfetched as that may seem.

Anyway, with the help of two other composers who were in Buffalo at the time and who had computer know-how—Tom Constanten (of "Grateful Dead" fame) and Leigh Landy, who now lives and works in Holland—I plugged along, gradually accumulating quite a lot of material. But then the arrangement with the movie firm got murkier and murkier and I suspect, in retrospect, that it must have been really in trouble, both artistically and financially.

So far as I know, the movie was never made or even really worked on. I never got the rest of the money due me, but by this time I much preferred to have unquestioned control of the tapes, and this did come about. Thus, within a few months, I salvaged almost everything of interest either in *Electronic Sonata* or in one or another of the subsidiary tapes of *Midnight Carnival.* Maybe Ovid's intention was finally realized after all—a metamorphosis from film sound track to a large tape piece with quite explicit programmatic content and on to a total sound environment. The moral is, I suppose, answer long-distance calls and waste not, want not!

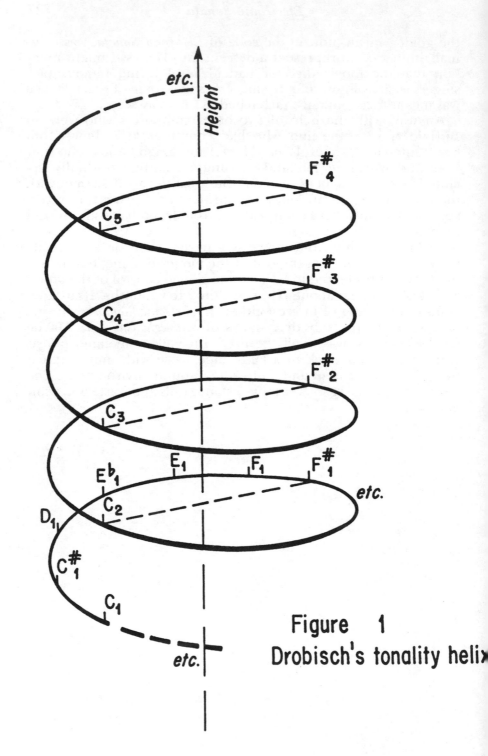

Figure 1
Drobisch's tonality helix

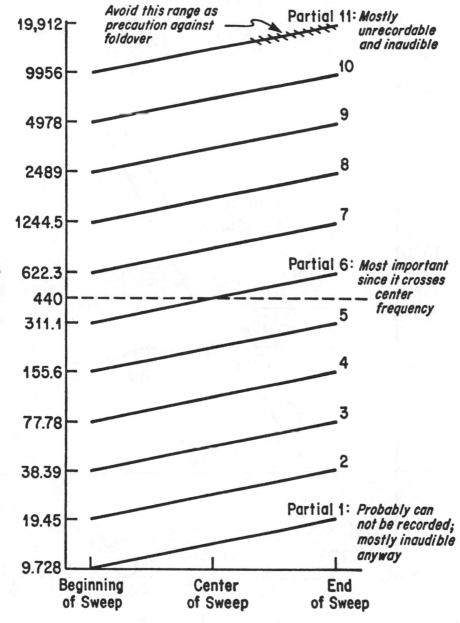

Figure 2 Basic plan of octave glissandi centered around concert A.

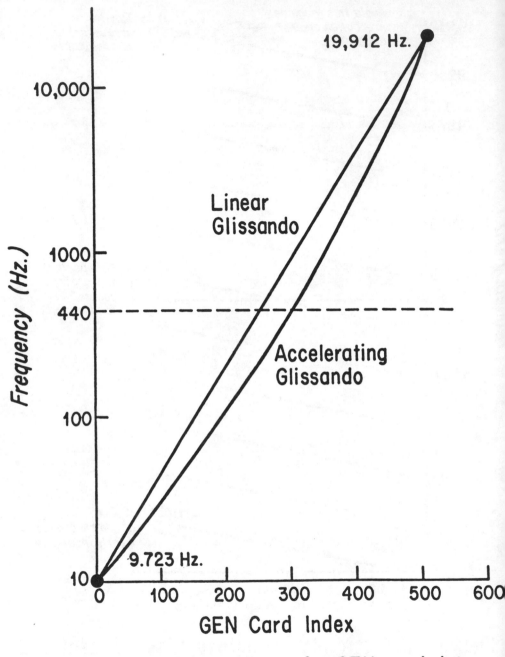

Figure 3 Frequency sweeps for GEN card data.

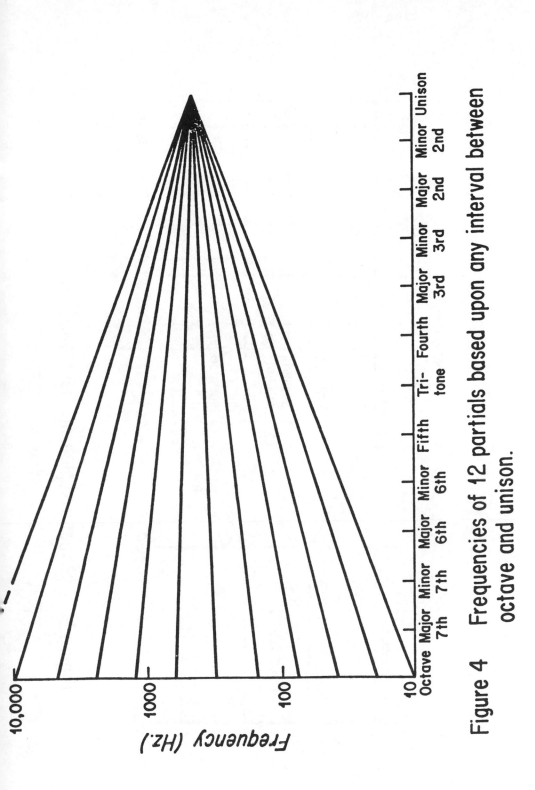

Figure 4   Frequencies of 12 partials based upon any interval between octave and unison.

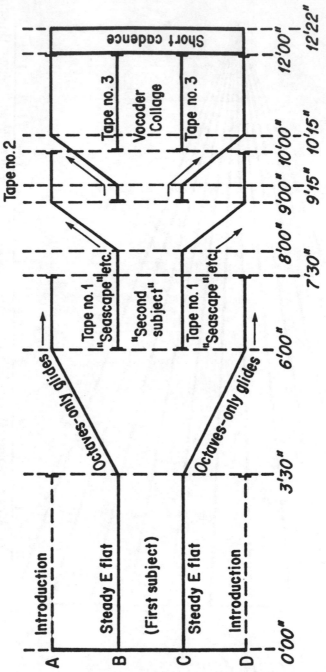

Figure 5   Structural plan of the exposition.

Composer's Input Outputs Music

Herbert Brün

UNIVERSITY OF ILLINOIS AT URBANA-CHAMPAIGN

It is one thing to search for events that will produce the sound one wants and quite another to discover the sound of the events one wants. In the first case, the wanted sound renders desirable the necessary events; in the second, the wanted events are the standard for the desirability of the resulting sound. These are not only two different approaches to the composition of music, but also two different political attitudes.

Even if it should be true that the great masters of the past only rarely considered political and social issues as criteria influencing their musical decision taking in composition, this truth should not simply be trusted. The actual concern of composers for their contemporary environment is usually less known than suspected. By now, many phenomena that until recently had been attributed to human frailty, to fate, or even to the laws of nature have been recognized as issues of political and social rather than individual and natural significance. Certainly no reliable documentation exists proving that any composer remained uninfluenced by these issues, as they appeared to him in his day, whether he knew it or not. All one is allowed to conjecture is that the less composers knew of the influence and the less they considered it, the more they became unconsciously dependent upon it.

The recent wave of growing awareness among artists and young people of the intrinsic unpleasantness that the systems we are caught in pour out over us with increasing generosity is an augmented version of the similar wave 150 years ago. It should delight the protesting intellect to contemplate the possibility of an amalgamation of a twentieth-century romanticism with the functional changes brought about by the existence of high speed electronic computers. For it would look promising, almost reassuring, if for once in history an attempt were underway to couple the newest ideas for a better world with the latest knowledge about its potentials.

Not surprising then that a few composers are beginning to look for answers to the following two questions: (1) Is it possible to incorporate the definition of a musical idea into a computer program in such a way that the program will generate the compositional realization of that idea? and (2) Is it possible to design a computer system and a computer program wherein a musical idea would function as a generator of systems so structured that the sequence of their states could be called a musical composition by the composer?

The quest for answers has already produced a long line of audible experiments, some of which, undertaken by composers, demonstrate the distinct possibility of a musical solution to the problem given. The composers I mean, of course, do not simply attempt to translate conventional techniques of composition into programming languages, nor are they interested in having the computer simulate traditional stylistic prejudices. They rather tend to start from scratch, to begin by stipulating what music is to be now that the assistance of computers has become available. As a necessary preamble to this quite deliberate act of stipulation, a composer has to understand that neither music nor computers grow wild in nature. Both, music and computers, are concepts referring to systems created by human beings. It should be obvious to the composer that, therefore, a new system has to be created, a system in which music and computers will mutually relate by analogy, by simulation, by structural correspondence, by exploitation of one another's information potential.

During several years of research in computer-assisted musical composition at the Experimental Music Studio of the University of Illinois,[1] many problems have been solved and new problems discovered. Our general approach to the field under investigation may grossly be described as the following three modes: (1) structural analysis and synthesis of compositional logistics and logics and their reduction to, or expansion into, computer programs; (2) analysis and synthesis of acoustical phenomena and their controlled and recorded production by a combination of A/D and D/A conversion processed and executed in computer systems; (3) attempts at an evaluation and the application of thoughts and ideas with regard to musical aesthetics and forms, created by the confrontation of the composer with technological conditions.

At various stages of this project the information already gained by that time was applied to specific purposes. The results are musical scores to be performed by musicians, tapes containing synthetic sound, and additions to the academic curriculum in musical education.[2] Every one of these results reflects on and illustrates the state of work in progress on any one or all of the modes of investigation mentioned above.

On the following pages I shall give an account of some thoughts and ideas that have been provoked by various aspects of the project. Not all of these thoughts and ideas deal directly with either music or computers; all, however, continuously accompany and strongly influence my work in research as well as in musical composition. To me these notions express the significance of hitherto latent and now, at last, emerging potentials far better than could many a less ambiguous, less polemic technical or theoretical report. The account will occasionally be interrupted by rather concise descriptions of musical works I composed with the assistance of computers.

*   *   *

The premise is that there be music. It is a deliberately stipulated premise. As such, it need not follow. It isn't even hereditary. That there was and is music proves, at best, that the premise has been deliberately stipulated many times before and that it has led to a variety of definite conclusions. The premise that there be music is not one of those conclusions. Now, to many a fine ear attached to many a fine brain, the premise, on the contrary, appears to claim: after all those conclusions, it may now be time that there at last be music. Only, however fine the attachments, however indignant the ear-wagging, and however shocked all those appear to appear who hear what only appears to have been said—it is all appearances only. The premise is not even a reaction. Nor is it the valiant expression of free and upstanding determination to start afresh, where there's a will there's a way, and finally succeed where hitherto all have failed. Nor does the premise stipulate that there should be better music or other music, but just that there be music! So the premise is not competitive either, and therefore does not necessarily signal the search for any social status or the embarking on some corrective action. In short, the deliberately stipulated premise that there be music is amoral, nonethical, nonconformist, and asocial, partly in contrast to whoever deliberately stipulates it. For he is not a premise, he only stipulates one. The urge to stipulate and the choice of premise are functions of his views on his participation in his society; and his views, be they affirmative or in opposition, are provoked, if not conditioned, by what happens in that society in the name of morals and ethics. Unfortunately, more often than not, he is a conformist. Instead of intolerantly discussing only the alternative consequences and conclusions that, given the premise, one now could envisage, again and again he allows himself to defend the premises against those who just do not want new premises. And he cannot be asocial, regardless of what he proclaims, in that he always finds himself either pooling with or pitching against society all those strange concepts his premise generates. No man is or does precisely what he intends to be or do. In various ways the environment attaches meaning and significance to man's expressions and actions which inevitably transcend and, in passing, deform all his intentions. This process occasionally creates a period in which man becomes all environment, and, unaware of this fact and hidden behind good intentions, he gets stuck. Whenever man gets stuck, the environment must be changed. An environment cannot be changed by obeying the environment, but only by experiments with deliberately stipulated premises that generate unexploited systems, moments of many alternatives. However, while man is caught in a feedback loop, he cannot recognize a loophole even if there is one because the foremost property of such a loophole is its imperceptibility. All he can do is to artificially increase the probability of his hitting on a premise that does more than he intended and so might catapult him out of the loop. Thus, it finally must be added that even the most deliberately stipulated premise lacks definition if one analyzes only the intentions it implies and that it mocks definition if it transcends all intentions.

SONORIFEROUS LOOPS (1964) for Flute, Trumpet, Double Bass, Xylophone, Marimba, Percussion, and Two-Channel Stereo Tape:
    The structure of the composition, defined by elements and rules, together with an algorithm which, in numerous passes (loops), operates in and on the structure as a generating function, was translated by the composer into two programs, one for the instrumental sections and one for the tape section. Both programs call on MUSI-COMP,[3] were written in SCATRE, and executed by the IBM 7094. The "instrumental" output, a printout, thus had to be recoded by the composer into a score and parts legible for live musicians. The "tape" output, a deck of punched cards, was converted into actual sound by the computer CSX-1 and stored on audio tape. The final performance tape is the result of extensive modifications on the CSX-1 sound,

achieved with the analog equipment of the Experimental Music Studio. The composition and programming of this work represent an attempt at coming to musical terms with two possibilities first offered to the composer by the computer: (a) random flight sequential choices channeled and filtered under the control of form-generating restrictive rules; this process created the shape, density fluctuations and parameter-details of the instrumental sections; (b) the transformation of speed of sound sequences into color and timbre of sound; this method was used for the production of the tape sections.

*   *   *

Though the act of deliberate stipulation may indicate (at least today) a gesture of defiance aimed at contemporary society's rules of etiquette in discourse; though it seems to condemn society's assumed competence in matters of communication to irrelevance and obsolescence: the premise so stipulated must not, in itself, contain either mood or character of such defiance nor betray any opinion of itself with regard to its relevance, its importance, or, just in general, its social and scientific value and meaning.

The premise has to appear in a statement, which becomes a false statement if the premise is taken to be a member of a set of conclusions based on any other premise. The statement should be true if and only if the premise is but a premise and thus, instead of following other premises, precedes consequences.

The premise must not be authoritarian but instead authorize a sufficiently large number of alternative possibilities of consequences. It has to require controversy among those who agree to test its potential for becoming the initial state of systems yet to be created. The controversial issue should not be which system, thus envisaged, deserves to be considered preferable but rather the rigorous analysis of patterns emerging in each such system and the recognition of patterns common to all.

The premise must not contain any answer to the question as to whether it be true or false. Its grammatical construction alone should already make it inaccessible to logical or intuitive function rules.

And so on! Even as it is, the manifesto of commandments invites the derisive shrugging of shoulders and sundry snide remarks referring the author to logics, beliefs, knowledges, maybe even to etiquette and better behavior. But most prominently among those turning their back, friends can be heard who would agree, were it not that they, unfortunately, cannot quite help having discerned and detected a contradiction or two, self-contradictory statements made in the tentative description of the conditions under which a premise may be awarded the distinction of being called deliberately stipulated. Unhappily, these friends are overly pedantic. Their regretful quibbling is nothing but a cautious gesticulation conforming to all those systems ruling us, in which self-contradictions, be they a person's or a thought's entanglement between reality and desire, are put down as flaws, mistakes, errors, fallacies, and considered inadmissable. It would be better, in fact it is necessary these days, for them to recognize that an enormous number of consistent individuals and ideas, causing one social disaster after another, remain uncontradicted for reasons that the systems we have accepted, or that at least rule us, consider admissible.

NON SEQUITUR VI (1966) for Flute, Violoncello, Harp, Piano, two sets of Percussion, and Two-Channel Stereo Tape:

For the instrumental parts here again a program written by the composer in SCATRE, calling on MUSICOMP, was executed by the computer IBM 7094, resulting in a printout that was recoded into score and parts for the musicians to read. The "tape" sections, however, were programmed by the composer for the new D/A sound synthesis system. The resulting sounds were used without modification just as the computer and converter system had synthesized it.

The programming of this work mainly reflects the continuous search for answers to the following: (1) What is the minimal number and power of restrictive rules that will select from random generated sequences of elements that particular variety of element-concatenations satisfying the conditions for either recognizable or stipulated "musical" forms and events? (2) Could a combination of stochastic choice rules with heuristic, multivalent, decision-taking procedures contribute an apparent "musical" coherence to a chain of changes of state in a structured system?

* * *

A particular system is defined by the number of elements it contains, by the number and kinds of algorithms that can function in this system, that can control the changes of state in this system and provide the entrance to and exit from the system. Such a definition refers only to the structure and thus to the information potential of a system. It neither implies the existence nor describes the nature of the elements. The definition actually reflects only an image that someone chooses to have; the image of that context in which, for him, a sequence of states or changes possesses relevance and significance. Systems are created by definitions. Definitions are created by people searching for relevance and significance in their own existence and in the existence of all or part of their environment. Without the concept of system, the concepts of relevance and significance are meaningless. But they are equally meaningless with regard to so-called universal systems, where everything is as it is and could not be otherwise because that is the way it is; "it" being everything. For anything to be of relevance to something, to be of significance to someone, a system has to be imagined and then to be defined. Only artificial systems will clearly show that they have been selected by choice, thus implying the intended rejection of other, equally possible, indeed, even equally reasonable, systems. Everyone will agree that the quantity of possible or reasonable systems that can be imagined far exceeds the number of those which could also be called desirable. On the other hand, very few people would willingly support the statement that a system may just then be the most desirable when it appears most "impossible," most "unreasonable." This statement reflects on a situation our present society has to cope with and therefore should recognize. Furthermore, out of all this there emerges an outline for the field of any relevant research in aesthetics.

Whether a stated concept corresponds to some truth can be verified by comparing its linguistic content with the linguistic contents in statements accepted as true. Whether a stated concept corresponds to some reality can be verified by comparing its linguistic contents with the linguistic contents in statements accepted as describing reality. The objects of aesthetics, however, are statements not to be compared, unverifiable statements. Where both truth and reality are in abeyance, but desire is not, that is where aesthetics sets up its deliberately stipulated values. If there is anything everlasting about aesthetics, then it is the delightfully fascinating temporariness of its objects. It is on desires that aesthetics thrive and not on fulfillments. Here then is one valid connection between aesthetics and the arts. Just like aesthetics, the arts deal rather with a statement of desire than of truth and reality, and just like aesthetics, the arts develop an allergic sensitivity against all that is already considered to be true or real. In pronounced contradiction to religion, the arts condemn to obsolescence the belief in what is said to have been true always and in what is to come later. Instead, through aesthetics, they forcefully make their contemporaries aware of what might be real and true now, regardless of belief and of recorded or predicted history.

Music, in its final appearance, as it arrives at the listener's ear, preserves at least traces of the processes by which it emerged from chaos. The composer, having to account for time, cannot entirely undo or even replace it. As time is the inexorable accountant of sequences, either the cause or the result of events being looked at one after another, music is an analogy to all systems looked at in time, and thus irrelevant to time's past. This does not imply that the past is irrelevant to any system looked at in time. Relevance does not necessarily function both ways. No matter how much I admire the past, it simply cannot care about me and my acts; and still, I have to acknowledge that the past not only has passed forever, but that it irreparably did happen. Thus the past belongs to truth and reality and not to the realm of desire. Music is stipulated, not as time's victim but as time's master.

PLOT FOR PERCUSSION
TOUCH AND GO
STALKS AND TREES AND DROPS AND CLOUDS (1967).
Three Pieces for Solo Percussion.

For each of the three pieces a FORTRAN program was written by the composer and run on the IBM 7094. The output tape contained the instructions for the CALCOMP PLOTTER to draw the score of symbols to be interpreted by the performer.

The "notation" in the scores makes use of a selected set of symbols provided by the CALCOMP Library in the installed system. The "language" consists in the distribution, size, and position of symbols on the page, in various modes of connectivity between the symbols, and a few rules prefacing each piece. The "language" aims at eliciting from the musicians a "musical" response, which combines instrumental action and coherent interpretation. With the help of the faculty and students of the Department of Computer Science, the composer is now developing a system of symbols specifically designed for musical requirements.

* * *

The composer of music is in a position to effectively initiate, in the system he creates, an algorithm analogous to the algorithm he would like to see initiated in the system that contains him. The task of aesthetics, be it the composer's or the listeners's, is to determine, speculatively, whether the analogy implies, at least structurally, events of contemporary relevance in the system called environment; whether the composer was motivated by a vision of what would be desirable processes in his contemporary society. It is not of primary importance for aesthetics whether everybody or even anybody agrees on the desirability of the processes implied by a work of art. This is rather the subject of political considerations. Political considerations, however, all too often remain without tangible substance, because the contemporary significance of individual acts and decisions is ignored and thus never properly evaluated. Any research of an aesthetic nature that fails to discover what at a given time is believed to be true and real and what at the same time is desired to be or become true and real instead, fails to give food to political considerations and thus, simply fails.

INFRAUDIBLES (1967). Composition of and with computer-synthesized sounds on tape.

A FORTRAN program, written by the composer and run on the IBM 7094, generates data to be converted into sounds on audio tape by the D/A system.

Substituting sequences of different single periods for the modulation of simultaneous frequencies, the composer is able to control the infrastructures of the event forming sounds just as precisely as the macroevents of his composition. Thus "pitch" becomes a result of composition. The same holds true for the concept of sound timbre. The differences between complex waveforms that are the results of instantaneous addition of amplitudes on the one hand, and the results of the periodic repetition of sets containing sequences of different single periods on the other hand thus become available to the composer as musical parameters.

* * *

The most dangerous person, the most terrifying daily human threat to human society, the most insidious law-abiding culprit forever protected by the legal fetishists of innocence, his secret accomplices, is the self-appointed moron. Not to be confused with the natural moron who, lacking intelligence, is incapable of thinking about knowledge, the self-appointed moron is he who recoils in terrorized modesty and complains of lacking communication whenever a thought he never had is proposed in word or script; who then cries, displaying well-faked gestures of frustration: "It's wrong it's bad it's nonsense!" which in translation means that to him it is neither customary usage nor his own. The self-appointed moron is he who makes himself believe, until he honestly believes, that interesting things have the property of being interesting, that things are capable of relating to him, of all people, of all things, if

only they would—please would—and who is incapable of relating
to himself—damn him. The self-appointed moron is successful in
but no good to society. To no good he successfully tries to use his
high social status as an argument for his personal value. To no
good he successfully uses his reputation of being a guardian of
culture as an argument in support of his definition of culture. To
no good he successfully mobilizes religion, enslaves logic, triv-
ializes experience, and exploits hope in order to propagate his
own allegedly innocent helplessness as it meets with his own
allegedly unintended propagation of war, murder, fraud. He is
successful, but his success is conspicuous for spelling failure, in-
justice, disaster. And for all the complexity and variety of such
unfortunate influences on social affairs, matters of state, and
human dignity, there is less cause for wonder to be found than
embarrassment. The self-appointed moron, though powerful, is
not a monster but rather an obedient servant: he shirks all responsibility for the rules he obeys simply by believing in them. He
believes in them so much that even an event he dislikes will find
his approval if it is a consequence of the rules in which he believes.
Rarely will it occur to him to doubt his belief, to doubt the rules.
He will rather denounce mankind for being intrinsically bad than
to suspect himself and his beliefs. Far too many political leaders,
heads of state, composers, poets, professors, bosses, critics, publishers, chairmen, judges, lawyers, doctors, parents, teachers, po-
lice officers make their living as self-appointed morons, as realists
who know better than to know better.

The only really valid excuse for them is their ignorance, a very
particular ignorance. They all have agreed, by convention, to
ignore the possibility of happiness being a desirable premise
rather than only a desirable consequence. Even the best among
them retreat into mumbled apologies as soon as an idea that
possesses them is questioned for reasonability. With liberally doc-
ile meekness, they confuse the social status of being called right
with the revolutionary action of demanding to become right.

All the arts, and among them also music, occupy a strange
position in this dirty mess. It does not matter much what has been
said and written and confessed about the arts: in one way or
another, the arts were always analogies to something of significance in their contemporary environment. Some intentionally,
some by mistake. Even if one were to grant equal significance and
relevance to intended and unintended analogies, even if one were
to observe that the arts are full of both, it is of importance to note

that only the realized intentions determine whether a particular analogy will become a work of art or not. There can be no "bad" art; but there may be "no" art if an artist or a composer fails in transforming the intentions of an analogy into poetry or painting or dance or music or . . .

When, that is the question, when will sound, organized or not, be music? And why, even if it were what it should be, should it be? There are answers to these questions, provided they are asked and provided anyone is around who likes answers even though these answers may not appeal to him, appeal to his craving for secure knowledge, or appeal to his educated sense of consistency and coherence and reasonable argument. One such answer, for example, might run as follows: Sound will turn into music if the concatenations of its appearance follow a set of rules, which were, however, invented and deliberately stipulated by a social being. By someone who thus hopes to demonstrate and maybe even to render understandable to his environment his desire for a structure that has not yet been observed as possible in this environment. Any so stipulated structural premise, not permitted or warranted here and now, may generate a system of sound events that would be music because of its being analogous to structural possibilities envisioned as being permitted and warranted in some environment here, but later. And there should be music because of the composers today who are willing to take on the challenge of structural intricacies and information potentials of systems in sound that are compatible and thus capable of communication by analogy, with those social systems that rule our lives. For these composers the deliverately stipulated premise that there be music is a vital premise and a political necessity. Obviously, it would be without any substance, were it not that there is political significance to musical ideas. And that there is I now stipulate. For neither do I wish to see myself as a natural moron, who waits and waits for reality to confirm his notions; as if what was real could at the same time be a standard for what ought to be real. Nor will I settle for the role of the self-appointed moron whose hope and ambition it is to confirm reality. I contend it to be a real improvement that slowly people are beginning to note that there is political significance to musical ideas, just because musical ideas are deliberately stipulated premises; just because musical ideas can conjure up the analogy to a reality we are not yet caught up in, which has not yet warped our ability of committing ourselves to changes almost impossible to envision from where we stand now.

MUTATIS MUTANDIS (1968). Composition for interpreters.

A FORTRAN program written by the composer and run on the IBM 7094 generates instructions for the CALCOMP PLOTTER to draw various sets of figures.

The program simulates a process by which different shapes, each created independently and randomly somewhere on the page, appear to be mutations of one another. Seemingly uninterrupted chains of gradual transformations connect the shapes, thus suggesting a continuity that appears to cause the shapes but is actually caused by the shapes. The graphic displays turn into scores as soon as the interpreter translates their structural characteristics into the instructional code of another medium (music, movement, etc.) and following this translation recreates the simulated process by analogy.

* * *

The largest, most general, and thus most flexible systems man can control today are found among the electronic high speed digital and analog computer installations. The number of states representable by such machines is enormous; the elements, simple and semantically uncommitted, can stand for almost anything enumerable, quantizeable, measurable; the network potential offers the structural conditions for nearly any algorithm one can think of. Thus it is a system especially designed for utmost compatibility with all kinds of other systems, large or small, simple or complex, open or closed, numerical or logical. It is, therefore, up to the computer user to find or to construct the system in which his problems can be expressed and solved, in which the processes he desires to observe and test can be seen as chains of transformations. Once he has defined the system he needs, the user is able to plant it as a subsystem into the computer. This "planting" procedure is usually referred to as "programming."

A computer program is a set of instructions. If fed into the computer system in an appropriate code, the program communicates to the computer the structure, size, dimensions, rules, algorithms, etc., of a system that the computer system is to simulate. Under the control of such a program, the computer system will act as an analogy to the system that the programmer had in mind when he wrote the program. It is quite probable that not all composers think of their activities as being operations on and in systems, that not all processes leading to the final appearance of a musical work take place in only one or in any system. However that may be, the computer has to be programmed in order to be of any assistance, and a program can only be written by one who considers at least part of the work, the processes, and the data with which he is concerned as changes in and states of a system that he has defined.[4] The main problem thus appears at the beginning and again at the end of the entire proposition: Can the composer program musical ideas for a computer, and will the output of the computer contain musical ideas?

Notes

1. Computer-assisted musical compositions at the Experimental Music Studio, University of Illinois

    A. Lejaren Hiller and Leonard Isaacson, *ILLIAC SUITE* for String Quartet (1957).

    B. Lejaren Hiller, *THE FLYING LESSON* (from Music for *The Birds* by Aristophanes) (1958).

    C. Robert Baker, *CSX-1 STUDY* for Tape Alone (1963).

    D. Lejaren Hiller and Robert Baker, *COMPUTER CANTATA* (1963).

    E. Herbert Brün, *SONORIFEROUS LOOPS* for Five Instruments and Tape (1965).

    F. John Myhill, *SCHERZO A TRE VOCE* for Tape Alone (1965).

    G. Herbert Brün, *NON SEQUITUR VI* for Six Instruments and Tape (1966).

    H. Herbert Brün, *THREE PIECES* for Solo Percussion (1967).

    I. Lejaren Hiller, *ALGORITHMS 1* for Nine Instruments and Tape (1968).

    J. Lejaren Hiller, *AN AVALANCHE for Prima Donna, Pitchman, Player Piano and Percussionist* (1968).

    K. Herbert Brün, *INFRAUDIBLES* for Tape Alone (1968).

    L. John Cage and Lejaren Hiller, *HPSCHD* for Keyboard and Any Number of Tapes (1968).

    M. Herbert Brün, *MUTATIS MUTANDIS,* Graphics for Interpreters (1968).

    Student Compositions:

    A. Gary Grossman, *FOUR STUDIES for Illiac II* for Tape Alone (1966).

    B. Frank Moore and Michael Ranta, *Piece for Jazz Set* (1966).

    C. Michael Ranta, *Algol Rhythms* (1967).

    D. James Cuomo, *Zetos 1–5:* Five Compositions for various groups of instruments (1967).

    E. Neely Bruce, *FANTASY* for Ten Winds, Percussion and Tape (1967)— only in parts a computer generated score.

2. For example: Music 320, Composition of Music with the Assistance of Computers. Under this title I inaugurated a two-semester seminar in 1966 designed to inform composition students about possibilities offered and the problems posed by modern technology. An introduction to various aspects of computer systems and logistics was followed by the discussion of programming procedures and languages. An elementary instruction in using SCATRE and FORTRAN enabled the students to write short programs and run them on the IBM 7094. From here on it became possible to compare composition logic, as

they had learned and applied it before, to programming logic, and to discuss the conditions of compatibility between one and the other. The problem of translating musical ideas into a program was investigated and the influences discovered, which the availability of powerful algorithms and systems control might exert on the conception of musical ideas. As a result of this seminar, students proceeded to write programmed compositions, some of which are noted above.

3. *MUSICOMP* = Music—Simulator—Interpreter—for—COmpositional—Procedures.

Written by Lejaren Hiller and Robert Baker, MUSICOMP was the first compiler program in SCATRE for the IBM 7094 at the University of Illinois. This compiler accepted subroutines for various compositional problems; it was constantly improved and augmented by composers.

4. *SAWDUST* (Computer project music). The computer program that I called SAWDUST allows me to work with smallest parts of waveforms, to link them and to mingle or merge them with one another. Once composed, the links and mixtures are treated, by repetition, as periods, or, by various degrees of continuous change, as passing moments of orientation in a process of transformations.

A. *DUST* (1976)   10'30"
Not only old stuff but also the temporarily left alone collects dust. The dust collected offers a sensitive surface to a sensitive finger: the moving touch leaves traces.

B. *MORE DUST* (1977)   12'45"
Four times *MORE DUST* traces, interrupted by lost patience, an eight-voiced statement that remains unachieved. To seemingly dust a real surface is part of a communication, which turns, in search of the missing link, to the listener.

C. *MORE DUST with Percussion* (1977–78)   13'20"
Listen, how Three face, confront, play up to it. And say, Listener. Don't we all?

D. *DUSTINY* (1978)   5'30"
First Composition; then, for instance, Music. Set, Link, Mingle, Merge, Vary: Play! First distinctly now; then, temporarily, for instants.

E. *A MERE RIPPLE* (1979)   11'36"
One sequence is varied fifty-six times, with exclamatory admonishments to itself thrown in and between. (This music does not speak for itself.) *A MERE RIPPLE* likes neither its composer nor its listener. Least of all it likes the learned who know what's what. It wouldn't mind, however, if all this were to change and would rather be swallowed by change than be liked without. (This music does not want to speak for itself lest it discourage someone from speaking for it.)

F. *U-TURN-TO* (1980)   6'00"
The tale of how three ear-training gestures, mere shadows of what once they had been, stubbornly keep dancing, each gradually accumulating its corps de ballet, and how they, according to conceivable concepts of aesthetics, keep getting both here and nowhere. *U-TURN-TO* means: only a swift and sudden, often forbidden, U-Turn (and that To), might let us see, for a fleeting

moment, the mug of the crook who makes and breaks the laws that we may neither break nor make but must, against better knowledge, defend.

G. *I TOLD YOU SO* (1981)   13′00″
    Like many other deadly stupid phrases, this one also seems too tough to be silenced. So I buried it alive.

These tapes are available through Lingua Press, P.O. Box 3416, Iowa City, Iowa 52244.

Fire and Ice: A Query

Priscilla McLean

A new auditory phenomenon has emerged with the birth of music produced by the tape recorder and synthesizer (electronic, musique concrète). It could be described as a sonic experience that is neither a continuation of the traditional abstractions (melodic-rhythmic groupings with timbres and textures as primary or secondary considerations) nor "kidnapped" environmental aura but a sonorous occurrence somewhere in between. For example, much electronic music seeks to imitate various musical instruments via the synthesizer or uses recognizable sounds from the environment (birdcalls, whale songs, radio communiqués, etc.). These sounds are then altered, but the actual source or intended imitation is still clearly perceptible. Also recently explored is a sound that is removed several degrees from any obvious source onto a more abstract level, either by altering the original drastically as to obliterate any direct reference to it or by synthesizing a musical event reminiscent of an environmental sonority but on its own level of abstraction. This imago-abstract sound, often gestural in nature, evokes dual sets of realities and is often misinterpreted by listeners and composers, who tend to react with suspicion and hostility toward electronic music of this kind.

In an article entitled "Toward Good Vibrations," Charles Wuorinen draws the basic premise that the imprecisions and generalities of exactly notated music, which implicitly demand the "performers' interpretation and projection" present problems for electronic realization and that many composers in the electronic medium, instead of creating a more precise, clear unfolding of the structures, confuse and blur the network of relations by using more generalized noise-oriented (not pitch-rhythmic) sounds and concentrating on the sound-events themselves (called "things" by Wuorinen) rather than their interrelations.[1] He states that the relations "enable us to identify the things" and then explains that the sounds themselves are "just arrays of vibratory relations." Many composers of electronic music, according to Wuorinen, are unaware of the overgenerality of their musical structures and hence the great variety of meanings inherent in them. These "failures" have resulted in "gross structural defects" and, Wuorinen states, formally unsatisfactory electronic music.

The opinion that workable ideas be "abstract" pitch-rhythmic manipulative entities in electronic music and that less malleable sonorities, either locked into a sound-event coalescence of pitch-rhythm-texture-timbre, as in the "wild bull" sound of Morton Subotnick's *The Wild Bull*,[2] or derived or influenced by programmatic, environmental experiences, are "inferior" because of their suspected inability to form diverse and complex relationships, is held by not a few composers, critics, and (usually instrument-oriented) listeners. If the ability to form complex varied relationships *is* the pinnacle of musical achievement, are imago-abstract sounds valid as workable sources, or are they to be restricted to dramatic gestural, usually superficial effects, used sparingly, if at all?

A constrasting stance to the view expressed by Charles Wuorinen is found in the music and writings of Jon Appleton. The sound sources of several of his works have come from the urban environment, generally derived from different communicative situations among people. The sound materials, whose origins remain recognizable, are then put through several formal variations, repetitions, additions, and alterations via tape and synthesizer manipulation to produce a completed work of musique concrète. For example, one work entitled *Chef d'Oeuvre* is a kaleidoscope of electronic manipulations of a singing commercial for frozen pizza, with the "pizza" still intact.

Appleton is concerned with a somewhat different aesthetic than has been heretofore presented: the use of sound objects as recognizable referents and as musical gestures invoking other levels of meaning, attributable to the previous information the sounds contained (the singing commercial), in combination with the new meanings created by the electronic and formal alterations. Appleton states: "Consequently one idea, the most obvious example being the human voice, can express either level or both simulta-

neously. The ambiguity that results from this use of sound produces a tension which is resolved by our aesthetic comprehension
or our sense of humor."[3]

The balancing of interrelations of the musical ideas involves a
basic compositional skill; the connotations of the nonabstrac-
tiveness of the sounds involve more varied responses. When the
original information is still clearly recognizable, the listener's responses are perhaps not so different from responses toward program music. Reactions to Appleton's approach have not all been
positive. One critic summed up his *World Music* as "a mish-mashed
melange of travelog sounds."[4]

There is a third viewpoint, which lies somewhere between those
expressed by Wuorinen and Appleton and takes advantage of the
characteristics of each. The imago-abstract sound, if created with
consideration of its manipulativeness, can be capable of many
levels of interrelation, according to its abstract qualities and also
connotative meanings evoked by the degree of allusion to other
sound images. The important thing here is that this kind of sound
is unique in its own sense, and not a direct recognizable referent—
it has a characteristic quality not unlike a motive or theme (and in
fact may use these), with only vague reference to alluded sonic
events.

One has only to listen to *Visage* by Luciano Berio to hear how
this works. In this landmark imago-abstract composition using the
voice of Cathy Berberian with electronic sounds, there is only one
actual work spoken: "Parole". The basic components of speech—
syllables of vowel and consonant combinations extracted from
several languages and recombined into nonsense sounds—are
joined with a great variety of dramatic vocal gestures, alternating
and mixing with electronic materials. The effect of these vocal
gestures is quite provocative: the nonwords expressed with such
strong inflections first stimulate the listener into imagining an
intelligible dramatic monologue, and later into perceiving the
sounds for what they are; an artwork of interweaving complex
vocal abstractions. The listener's focus fluctuates between these
levels of comprehension, invoking the tension that Appleton suggested without being able to evoke an actual verbal or programmatic image, since only one real word is used,[5] and this word
conveys little imagery in itself.

This powerful dramatic work of Luciano Berio seems to be a
refutation of Wuorinen's argument that nonpitched material cannot form strong syntactical relationships. And yet the implied or
imagined origin is also there in strong measure. It is the combina-

tion of these supposedly opposing forces that gives the work its unique power.

The imago-abstract sound works well in combination with more abstract ideas, as boundaries between the two are broken, and at times the allusions or suggestiveness of the sounds seem to leap out in bold relief, playing with one's cognitive abilities. Since 1971, when I started working in the electronic medium, I have become intrigued and fascinated with this multirole of imago-abstract sounds and in *Dance of Dawn*[6] have used them in dramatic gestural and structural ways interwoven with abstract ideas. In spite of the title, the work is not programmatic (the title and poem came after the composition was finished), and none of the sonorities are meant to be programmatic.

To illustrate how one of the principal imago-abstract ideas—a nontempered melodic contour that is ululatory in timbre and character—functions in *Dance of Dawn,* I have prepared a loose diagram of its appearance and development throughout the twenty-two minute work (see fig. 1.).

Explanations of Symbols in Figure 1

A1: Imago-abstract sound (functioning here as introductory, gestural).

A2: Variation and extension in two voices, enhancing the progression of the pitch-rhythmic abstract ideas occurring at this time.

A3: Slight variation of A1 sound, introducing new section after earlier climax.

A4: Repetition of A1.

A5: Duet of A1 variations (high and lower pitch levels) occurring during a new melodic section, promoting continuity, unity.

B1: Strongly dramatic, gestural (similar in dramatic upsweep to A1), heralding climax and long pause at first "half" of work.

B2: Repetition of B1 with A variation, beginning second half.

B3: Extension of B1, in duet with A6 (high variation and extension of A1), beginning a section that is "recapitulatory."

C: Similar to B3 in timbre and dramatic intent, climaxing this section.

A7: Return of the original imago-abstract sound in multiple variations polyphonically (in its most intricate form) closing the work.

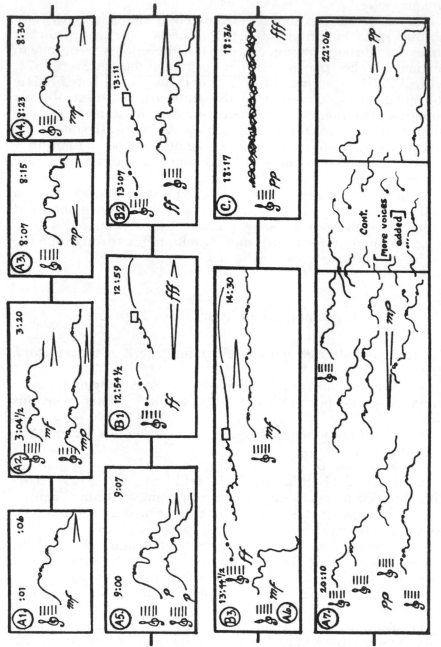

Fig. 1

As the diagram illustrates, the sound-event is as much a part of the intrinsic structure of the work and as complex interrelationally as are the totally abstract sounds (if there is such a thing as "totally abstract"); it also serves the important function of delineating sections. I did not notate specific pitches in the diagram, since the pitches are a mixture of tempered and untempered (microtonal) tones; in this piece, the contour and shape of the "melodic line" are more important than its exact pitch content. Because this sound-event is basically an evocative, dramatic gesture, and hence quite memorable, caution was needed not to overuse but to take advantage of its character by placing it in structurally strategic locations. In this way, the imago-abstract sound was able to create unity and coherence while evoking several simultaneous auditory responses. Although only one sound-event has been isolated for analysis, there are other imago-abstract events throughout *Dance of Dawn* that often evolve to and from completely abstract sound patterns.

This way of imagining and treating musical ideas seems to be a direct consequence of the development of electronic equipment and technique. Early musique concrètists often manipulated pre-existing sounds via tape recorder and record player. When synthesizers became available, concrète sounds were (and are) altered in various ways electronically; and thus emerged the phenomenon of "distorted" sounds as found in the music of Jon Appleton. Whether the new way of hearing and examining existing sonorities and altering them or creating new ones directly influenced the sonic extensions presently available on conventional (and unconventional) instruments, or whether this creative expansion began on its own is not clear, but there seems to have been mutual interest and development in all areas of musical expression. This is of course understandable, since many composers are writing both in electronic as well as vocal and instrumental media, and most composers have at least studied or tried the different combinations.

The development of the electronic devices—tape recorders, synthesizers, sequencers, and recently computers—has become more and more sophisticated and has given the composer the ability to create the imago-abstract sound. As the concept began and was integral to concrète music, so it has matured in its capacity to work at both the abstract level as well as its intrinsic derived level.

Perhaps Charles Wuorinen and others in agreement with him could benefit by this quotation from Henri Pousseur, who, in discussing the evolution of order in music, had this to say about the present developments, as well as the future:

> I would even hazard the prediction that evolution in the near future will be in a direction such that all types of musical expression known up to the present will be made usable again (along with other, entirely unknown types relating to other domains of our auditive experience). . . . The most probable and legitimate natural consequence of such a widening of expression would be the ability of new music to reach vaster auditive capacity; and the possibility of its finally achieving the major mutation in collective sensibility which it carries within it in embryonic form.
>
> . . . [Form] is not called on to explain the whole of reality once and for all, but to make as vast a space as possible inhabitable for us—the largest of which we are capable. It is not enough for us to alter the "exterior" world in order to accomplish this, but also—above all, perhaps—*ourselves*, our attitude, and our "resonance" (like a violin's, a filter's, an antenna's).[7]

Notes

1. Published originally in the journal *Prose* and excerpted in Elliott Schwartz's *Electronic Music: A Listener's Guide* (New York: Praeger 1975), pp. 256–60.
2. Nonesuch Records 71208.
3. *The World Music Theatre of Jon Appleton.* Sounds and electronic tape, Folkways FTS 33437.
4. Levering Bronston in *The New Records,* H. Royer Smith Co., October 1975, 12.
5. *Parole:* French for "speech".
6. Composers Recordings, Inc., SD 335
7. "The Question of Order in New Music," *Perspectives on Contemporary Music Theory,* Benjamin Boretz and Edward T. Cone, eds. (New York: W. W. Norton, 1972), pp. 114–15.

'Otahiti: The Evolution
of a Personal Style

Jon H. Appleton
DARTMOUTH COLLEGE

In 1963, while a graduate student at the University of Oregon, I composed one of my first pieces of electronic music, called *Primary Experience*. I recorded the voices of school children in speech and song and the sounds of children's games. I brought this material to the primitive collection of audio equipment we called our electronic music studio. I edited the materials, made loops of phrase fragments, mixed in the sounds of bells and vibraphone, and created a haunting collage which made some listeners feel as though they were hearing memories of their own childhood. I was certainly influenced by Stockhausen's *Gesang der Jünglinge* (1955–56), but my work had quite a different character and was, by comparison, extremely unsophisticated.

In 1965, while working at the Columbia-Princeton Electronic Music Center I recorded the voices and cries of infants and used this material as the basis for a work called *Infantasy*. I modified the voices in various ways and extended their cries by adding pitched material from oscillators, which I matched to the infant sounds as closely as I was able. By working with the cries at slow speeds I discovered two interesting effects. Firstly, where I thought the infant was catching her breath, there were faint tails of the cry which were so high in pitch as to be normally inaudible. Secondly, the sobbing of a frustrated baby became a hideous and terrifying adult male cry at slower speeds. Listeners often remembered the name of the piece as *Infanticide* instead of *Infantasy*. I imposed certain rhythmic gestures by splicing together "cry phrases," and this gave the work some momentum.

155

Infantasy had a simple form: it began abstractly, moved through sections where the voices were partially identifiable, and ended with a repeated pathetic infant whimper that grew larger and deeper with each repetition. The process of moving in and out of realistic sounds and sound situations seemed to me a useful "form" to develop, and between 1963 and 1973 I used this technique in eighteen different pieces.

The most popular electronic piece I have composed, *Chef d'Oeuvre*, was my first composition after opening the electronic music studio at Darmouth College in 1967. This work had as source material a "singing" radio commercial by the Andrews Sisters for Chef Boy-ar-Dee frozen pizzas. I suspect that this piece succeeds because the audience gets caught in a snappy, syncopated rhythm that propels some obviously electronic sonorities and then suddenly discovers that the same rhythm belongs to a slick and humorous musical style. The piece ends almost as precipitiously as it begins, and I intentionally tried to preserve the frantic pace of some radio commercials.

In 1969 I spent a week recording sounds in New York City: taxis and subways, harbor sounds, but also musical relics including old phonograph rolls and music boxes. When I returned to Vermont where I live, I was struck by the contrasting silence which was broken only by small frogs called "spring peepers." I immediately wanted to use all these sounds and a program occurred to me: a temporal and geological cross section of New York, starting with the present at street level and descending in space and time, down through the pavement to the cellars and subways, to the graves of forgotten Broadway comics, and finally to forgotten civilizations. The end of the piece was a return to the stillness of the "spring peepers" which I reached through a subway train that is transformed into a space and time vehicle. I called the piece *Times Square Times Ten*. People told me that I was composing "films for the blind," but the musical events were more compressed and less specific than one finds on a film sound track.

I began to build a large library of sounds and sound situations by recording everywhere I went. Once I was stranded at the Newark Airport on the way to a concert in North Carolina. The airport lounge was packed with travelers, and I interviewed them all, asking "What do you think of the new electronic music?" *Newark Airport Rock* was a piece made of their answers to my question with appropriate musical accompaniment.

At this time I became interested in using the sounds of exotic musics, instruments, and voices as source material. Most of the material I collected myself: the Swedish *nyckelharpen,* the sounds of a Turkish village, and even the voices of airline attendants while I was traveling. The sounds suggested moods and situations, which I tried to translate into musical pieces. When I could not physically go someplace, I did so electronically by telephone and by borrowing the recordings others had made. One piece, *Sones de San Blas,* consisted of a musically-illustrated telephone call to Mexico, including the sounds of the equipment and telephone operators trying to locate a coastal village. Another piece, called *CCCP* used Russian folk music and an ancient recording of a reading by Leo Tolstoy.

To accompany a piece of sculpture by Varujan Boghosian I composed *Hommage to Orpheus.* The sculpture suggested a large religious icon of unidentifiable origin. I wanted the musical sources to be equally evocative but unknown. I mixed together the chanting of an African "Christian" cult called the Bwiti with a synthesized chant. The former had been recorded by anthropologist James Fernandez.

In 1971 I began to express political ideals in my electronic music. In an effort to unseat the former director of the Swedish National Center for Electronic Music (Stiftelsen EMS), I composed a piece for the Swedish Text-Sound Festival called *Dr. Quisling in Stockholm.*[1] Later I collaborated with the American jazz musician Tom Scott on a piece using voices and sounds of the upheavals of the sixties. I used the voices of the astronauts together with those of Major Mat Matson (the Mattel toy astronaut) and Richard Nixon called *Apolliana.* These pieces are both of dramatic and musical interest. The political content tends to obscure the perception of them as musical compositions.

In 1972 I became interested in Polynesia. I wrote about this in an article entitled "The Electric Music of Tonga: The Use of Nonwestern Music by Western Composers."[2]

My interest in the music of the Kingdom of Tonga grew out of my work in comparative literature where I often had compared the ideas expressed by music and literature. Could one say that in Western civilization there are significantly different concepts expressed through the verbal and musical languages? . . . .

Friends and colleagues suspected that my research in Polynesia was simply a manifestation of what Robert Goldwater, writing of Paul Gaugin, called "geographical romanticism that has not yet lost its flavor, and has been made a symbol for the throwing off of the stifling superfluities of the hothouse culture of Europe in favor or return to that more natural way of life [of] which Rousseau is the generally accepted advocate." How can I deny that after weeks spent with a computer, producing music that "would appear to be for, of and by specialists" that any composer might yearn for a less complicated and more rewarding musical environment?

Gauguin, Debussy, and more recently Harry Partch have written about the influence of nonwestern art on their work. Partch wrote:

> From one standpoint the twentieth century is a fair historical dupli-
> cate of the eleventh. At that time the standard and approved eccle-
> siastical expression failed to satisfy an earthly this-time-and-this-place
> musical hunger; result the troubadours. Today, and especially in
> America, the approved Abstraction is a full musical fare for only a
> small percentage of our people, and the resulting hunger is satisfied
> by anything that breaks the formal barriers in the direction of Cor-
> poreality-hillbilly, cowboy, and popular music, which, whatever its
> deficiencies, owes nothing to scholastic and academic Europeanisms.[3]

There are large differences between composers who are inspired by nonwestern music, those who incorporate some of its techniques (Steve Reich) and those who use nonwestern music as source material. Unfortunately, I tried to do all three things in my first "Pacific" piece, *Ofa 'atu Tonga,* and it didn't work. In 1974, an opportunity arose that led me to compose what I believe to be the best piece in the genre I have described above, *'Otahiti.*

An invitation came to compose a piece in the studios of the Group de Musique Expérimental de Bourges, France. I had recently returned from the Pacific, where France had resumed the testing of nuclear weapons near Tahiti, and I had a good collection of Polynesian music and sounds as source material. The following is a chronicle of the sonic content of *'Otahiti,* together with a personal afterview of its programmatic content.

Time   *Contents*

0:00   From silence, a very low, quiet melodic pattern played on a
         conch-shell trumpet, lowered by two octaves, suggests the
         primeval past. Continues until 1:47.

0:10   "Insects," electronically generated, very high in pitch, come
         and go between channels and by contrast to the low
         trumpet define a large empty space. The feeling of being

on a Pacific island looking out to the horizon. "Insects" indicate the presence of life-forms on the island.

1:11   A steady, high pitch, derived from the insect sounds appears suddenly, introducing a fragmented Tahitian chant ("Chant in the Face of Danger"), partially ring-modulated so as to appear sufficiently distant in time and only partially comprehensible. Above the low trumpets, and under the voices is heard the conch-shell trumpet at correct pitch, untreated.

1:47   Previous activity stops, and from the distance the conch-shell trumpet pattern begins anew at normal pitch, coming to the foreground and implying a move to the present time.

1:56   A chant "'ea, 'ea," is clearly heard. The voice belongs to an old man and moves between channels, with different reverberation periods, alternating at increasing speed with the trumpet melody. It is dramatically interrupted.

2:23   Explosion of an "atomic bomb." A sudden, very loud square wave is heard with high pitch, slow, downward glissandi followed by a modulated triangle wave pulse suggesting radiation. A second glissando is heard as the bomb effect dies away.

2:53   Silence. All life-forms seem to have vanished.

2:55   "Insects" reappear slowly. The listener does not know what other life-forms will reappear. This continues until 3:55.

3:15   As though all is forgotten, a soft, electric guitar riff, with light, trap-set accompaniment, emerges and is played in canon. The melody is Hawaiian ("Aloa, aloa") but is an example of commercialized music in Tahiti today, sometimes called "airport art." It is meant to contrast with the earlier chant and to signify the arrival of foreign interests in Tahiti. Above the tune appears a short melodic counterpoint, which derives from the "radiation" glissandi. It is intentionally trite so as to enhance the commercialism of the tune itself. All this fades, but continues until 4:44.

4:25   "Hallo?" The telephone is answered by a Frenchman, who portrays the French Minister of Atomic Energy. We hear only his part of the conversation, in French, in which he assures the caller that radiation is actually beneficial to the health of "our little friends in the South Pacific." The call continues until 5:12.

4:47   A shout is heard under the conversation and begins a long passage of Tahitian drumming ("tiaré taporo"), a traditional dance accompaniment, which slowly builds in volume.

5:12   The drumming comes to the foreground. New layers of drumming are introduced. Each successive layer has the same rhythm but is faster and higher in pitch. The amplitude of the entire passage increases until it changes character from entertaining to grotesque and frightening. It *becomes* another explosion.

6:08   An explosion, with radiation tails, suggests again the destruction of the Tahitians. There are cries heard under the explosion this time.

6:21   As the explosion subsides, a three-note motive emerges—a kind of melancholy plea.

6:33   A light "Dance of the Children,"[4] played by a guitar, is electronically processed so as to make it brittle. It serves as a background to the three-note motive. The motive is developed and becomes part of the guitar texture. This continues until 7:44.

6:54   A low horn, as though heard from the harbor, suggests a ship moving out to sea. It brings a sense of sadness to this part of the piece, a feeling of resignation.

7:03   The horn again.

7:19   The horn again.

7:44   The guitar fades into a layered pattern of repeated pulses, each layer at a different pitch and speed. The section suggests a suspension of the action, a movement to another time. This continues until 8:21.

8:04 A Tahitian monotonic chant, called "Geneology,"[5] is transformed by pitch modification, suggesting the indomitable spirit of the Tahitians in the face of the foreign invasion.

8:09 An answer to the chant and the return of the "insect" sounds.

8:21 A low, reverberant thud, a note of finality, suggests the elimination of military domination.

8:23 A pathetic priest chanting a distorted "Gloria" is answered by another chant fragment.

8:37 A second low, reverberant thud suggests the elimination of religious domination.

8:45 The chant resumes with a slightly more optimistic and timeless feeling.

8:54 Another, low, reverberant thud signals the end of the story. The "insects" swirl about and finally disappear.

9:06 End.

As I indicated above, I began to compose *'Otahiti* with only a very general program in mind. By working with the materials in a purely musical way, certain specific content suggested itself. The construction of the piece was improvised but then tightened as the composition progressed. Many of the programmatic ideas expressed above were not consciously introduced but were discovered later on listening to the piece. Most of these ideas have been understood by others without my explanation. I do not think the piece needs my specific interpretation to succeed, but the general idea must be perceived. This is a requirement of all "program" music and considered by some to be a limitation.

In the Spring of 1977, my wife Elisabeth (who teaches dance at Dartmouth College) and I choreographed *'Otahiti* with a young dancer who knew traditional Polynesian dances. The effect of the dramatized version was quite different from listening to the piece alone. Some of it became didactic and the references proved to be too specific.

At the present time I feel that I have exhausted the musical genre described here. It has led my work in two opposing directions: toward traditional electronic music and toward musical-dramatic works combining dance and electronic music.

Notes

1. A discussion of this work is contained in *Electronic Music: A Listener's Guide* by Elliot Schwartz (New York: Praeger Publishers, 1975), p. 202.

2. Jon H. Appleton, in *Mundus Artium* 7 (1974): 172.

3. Harry Partch, *Genesis of a Music* (New York: De Capo Press, 1974), p. 52.

4. From *The Gauguin Years: Songs and Dances of Tahiti*, Nonesuch, H-72017.

5. Ibid.

Loudspeakers and Performers: Some Problems and Proposals

Dexter Morrill

COLGATE UNIVERSITY, NEW YORK

Perhaps some confusion has resulted in recent years from the continued use of the words *computer music* and *electronic music* to describe the medium in which many of us work. Indeed, Max Mathews's title for his paper, "The Computer as a Musical Instrument,"[1] may have seemed appropriate at the time but suggested that our new music should be defined according to the means of signal generation rather than according to the transducer, which has always been the loudspeaker. The term *synthesizer* does not help us much either. In 1981 the differences among devices that generate sources for loudspeakers are growing less obvious and less important. Soon we may realize that we are working in a loudspeaker medium, regardless of how the signals for the loudspeakers are generated. Musicians working in real time and in performance using computers, synthesizers, and circuits might rather think of themselves as loudspeaker performers. During the 1970s we witnessed a revolution in the technology of loudspeaker music. Thousands of pieces have been composed for tape alone and for tape and performers. Those of us who were working ten years ago have seen an incredible number of musicians and researchers begin to work in the tape medium.

What problems are encountered with the use of loudspeakers in musical performance? The problems I will discuss here are nontechnical and are limited to the use of loudspeakers where performers do not control the sound-generating equipment directly. Many of the ideas expressed in this article have grown out of my experience in performance over the past five years, first with a purely quad-tape program called *Rotations,* which I began doing in 1975, and later with a performer-tape series of programs called *Singing Circuits.* My awareness of the problems of using loudspeakers in performance began after 1978, when the newness of the "computer music" medium had worn off somewhat, and I had repeated the *Singing Circuits* program many times. During the early part of 1975 I decided to spend part of my time performing my own "computer" music and that of some other composers. I felt it was important to see that this music went forward with some care and direction, and I was already very unhappy with the "electronic" music concerts that I had heard. Too often, the equipment for these programs was inadequate or the programs poorly constructed, and both music and composers suffered. I decided to organize my own equipment for concerts and to put together a basic program of music whose organization could begin to compete with more conventional programs. Whenever possible I would travel to a concert with my own equipment even if only one of my pieces was to be performed.

By definition, *loudspeaker composers* take on much of the performer's role because the music is fixed in some important ways. Because at least part of the piece is often stored on tape, the composer must find a way to add what is normally the performer's information. This task can slow down the composing process. The loudspeaker instrument through which the music is realized for an audience remains somewhat passive unless the composer can be actively involved with the equipment during each performance. We need to exert some control over the performance of our tapes, much as performers control the output of their instruments.

The next five years will be critical ones for loudspeaker composers. Few resources and little money are available, our medium is no longer new, and we will need to demonstrate for our colleagues some good results if we hope to have their continued support. While the cost of hardware is declining rapidly, the overall cost of maintaining good studios will never be cheap.

Social Factors and Performance Spaces

Some obvious improvements have been made in loudspeaker design over the past ten to twenty years. The commercial music industry has contributed to the development of recording techniques, and our understanding of equalization and concert hall acoustics has grown. The proliferation of loudspeaker uses is staggering. It has been used to broadcast antisocial ideas, advertising, social anger and frustration, pleasure, and even social healing. The loudspeaker invades our privacy constantly. It can be hidden, purchased at very low cost, and can have enough acoustic power to kill a human being. The loudspeaker may also represent the end of music that is often described as heroic. All of these facts about loudspeakers relate to the social implications of their use—implications that have a direct bearing on how composers use loudspeakers in performance.

Many musicians in the 1960s looked forward eagerly to the construction of new performance spaces. *New music,* as most widely defined, needed new spaces desperately. This expectation, for the most part, was never met. There are very few good spaces in Europe and the United States for the performance of new music. We may even be stepping backward in this respect; some new university music buildings have worse halls than were formerly available. What is available to musicians using loudspeakers are conventional spaces, usually proscenium stages, meant for frontal and conventional heroic performances. We cannot ignore these spaces if we expect to perform often, even though the loudspeaker is at a disadvantage in them. Problems regarding performance spaces are also faced by musicians performing much of the historical repertoire.

The Question of Balance

I can vividly remember doing a concert of computer music at Colgate several years ago that consisted of some tape pieces and some pieces for performers and tape. The program began with two beautiful tape pieces and was followed by one that called for a performer. The audience reacted quite favorably to the first two pieces, but there was a sudden and noticeable increase in interest when the performer walked onstage. This phenomenon is well understood by most of us. It raises the question of roles and balance. My own guess is that in this mixed-media situation the performer commands about eighty percent of the audience's attention and the loudspeaker twenty percent. With supreme effort, the composer might equalize these percentages somewhat, but not much. Is there any reason to disturb this natural imbalance? I am not as interested in the imbalance itself as in the danger that we will end up composing a kind of "music minus one." This danger is rather great when we compose for loudspeakers and performers, and considerable thought is required to overcome it.

Performers often respond to poor balance by turning up the loudspeakers. At a rehearsal recently, I heard a very nice piece for tape, piano, and saxophone. The performers were frustrated with the balance between themselves and the tape and tried the ineffective solution of turning up the amplifier. Acoustic power is rarely the reason for lack of balance. We can easily identify an instrument played softly against some loud competing noises because, as listeners, we are trained to pick out performance cues. The brief but powerful cues found in the attack portion of many natural instrument tones enable us to find that sound and follow it within a complex acoustic event. This is not unlike the cocktail party effect, where we can easily follow the conversation of a single person. A possible solution to the balance problem is to lessen the acoustic power of the loudspeaker and to limit its musical activity to one voice. If, as composers, we can generate a high level of information in one voice that is a processed signal, we can begin to create on tape enough musical information to balance that supplied by live performers. Henry Brant points to the problem of balance in his writing about space and musical composition.[2] He suggests that loudspeakers have a concentrated and directional projection that is at odds with the diffused sounds made by live performers. Although Brant's reasons for proposing a maximum diffusion of sound are somewhat different from my own, his notion of an expanded spatial effect relates to the problems discussed here.

Perhaps we can achieve balance by measuring the musical activity of the players against that of the loudspeakers. A complex tape's texture and rhythmic activity suggest that the performer is a soloist who plays in a concerto role rather than in a more balanced musical one. We who compose in studios, hearing only the tape portion of a work for tape and performer, are probably going to err on the side of tape complexity if we are somewhat unhappy with the tape-performer balance.

Balance and Timbre

Most tape compositions are constructed with simple timbres. Often listeners are fooled when the sounds contain some unusual elements not heard before. But, too frequently, repeated hearings reveal that there is a low level of timbral information, and the music does not wear well. Although performers are not able to modify greatly many of the parameters that control their timbres, they do produce an enormous wealth of timbre information that may unfold rather slowly. Part of my initial and continuing excitement about using computers to generate acoustic signals is their great power in the area of timbre.

With Risset, Chowning, Grey, Beauchamp, Wessel, and others, I have felt that a natural task for composers of new music using computers is the study and synthesis of natural sounds. Our collective intuition was that we needed experience in simulating natural tones in order to build a solid base for unnatural or synthetic ones that we hoped would contain a high level of musical information. At least two other ideas are related to these interests: (1) the idea of interpolating synthetic timbres and (2) confusion between real and synthetic sound sources. My *Studies* for trumpet and computer (1975) were directed at timbral confusion and balance with a live trumpet player. In the past five years the progress made in timbre research has been significant, and there has been a high degree of interest in simulating and processing the human voice. Petersen's cross-synthesis techniques and the Bennett-Rodet CHANT voice programs at the Institute de Recherche et Coordination Acoustique/Musique have produced startling results. Compositions that feature timbres similar to those of live performers have a potential for balance that might not otherwise exist, especially if loudspeakers are placed with care. In the case of my *Studies,* I found it important to have the loudspeakers elevated to the height of the trumpet bell and to have both the loudspeakers and the player a good distance from the audience. Jean-Claude Risset's *Inharmonique* is marvelous for its balance of voice and tape, even without synthetic voice timbres in the tape part. The opening is especially interesting and is enhanced if the singer gradually walks toward center stage from a distance.

Recent timbre research has led to the study of larger questions about phrasing and other musical elements that are not contained in the single note. We are not very far along on this path, and the amount of information gained and its management pose significant problems. We know that performers demonstrate a personality or style at the level of the phrase and that this information is communicated well to audiences. If the music emanating from loudspeakers does not also communicate some higher-level information, balance will be hard to achieve. In at least one sense, our apparent need for higher-level information in sound synthesis suggests that timbre may not help much to achieve balance in the mixed, tape-performer medium and that composition may have to do this. We do not attend string quartet concerts and hear complaints that the quartets all sound alike. This is because audiences always focus on variety in compositions, even if the timbre of the four string instruments is only rich in information within well-defined limits. Very little can compensate for poor musical ideas in compositions. As composers, we need to be sure that our musical ideas are sufficient for achieving the tape-performer balance we desire. Even if we are sometimes discouraged about the hall, the placement of speakers, the quality of sound that each speaker imposes on all sounds passing through it, the limited dynamic range available, and a host of other limitations, we can always capture the attention of listeners by musical means. That is, we can shift listeners' focus or attention through composition. Good performers will want to contribute to our desired balance by not always being in the foreground.

Placement of Loudspeakers

The social and performance-space problems discussed earlier convince me that we cannot expect our concerts to be successful if we use a couple of ordinary loudspeakers, even if they are perfectly adequate to fill the room with sound and are of high quality. At least for the next few years, audiences will expect something special and unusual from our concerts, something that they feel they cannot hear in their own living rooms. If we place two speakers on a stage, audiences will form preconceived notions about what they are going to hear. An entire concert heard from speakers in one location can only be dull, and it is not much work to move them. It was established more than thirty years ago that to create a good stereo image the proper angle for two speakers is 30° from center.[3] Musicians still make the mistake of placing two speakers at the extreme right or left sides of a stage, thereby creating an enormous separation. In a large hall it is a good idea to use two or three speakers for each side and set them at different angles to the audience.

Musicians may want to use as many speakers as they can reasonably gather together and to place them in a variety of patterns. This does not mean that all of the speakers need to be used for each piece. If we are traveling with equipment, the limitations can be quite severe. But we might accomplish a good bit with a large number of very small speakers supported by two efficient woofers that can handle the low frequencies. Since low frequencies do not localize well, two woofers may be sufficient. We rarely attempt to raise speakers because this is often difficult. Yet it is often worthwhile. I constructed four six-foot portable stands from plastic plumbing pipe for my *Rotations* loudspeakers and found that the sounds were enhanced enormously. If we are going to be limited by frontal performance situations and constrained by time and resources, we should make every effort to achieve performance depth and height. Synthesis algorithms can create the feeling of depth through control of amplitude, reverberation parameters, and equalization of high and low frequencies for distance cues.

Composers do not use odd speaker arrangements often enough. Larry Austin has a delightful piece for viola and tape in which he uses one speaker. The limited dynamic range does not seem to be a problem, and I suspect that audiences may appreciate a piece that has a small and well-focused loudspeaker sound. Perhaps we should build sound equipment systems especially to meet our own performance needs. Planning and imagination can make up for the lack of expensive equipment. If we do not have a large power requirement, we should be able to use cheaper speakers and amplifiers chosen to work within a limited frequency range. In most cases, cheaper equipment produces acceptably low distortion if it is not operated at peak levels.

Conclusion

In this century we have expanded performance possibilities with equipment, and we have radically altered performance spaces. The elaborate sound system at Bourges (GMEBaphone) and the one designed by Varèse for the Brussels World Fair are two successful examples. Twentieth-century compositions frequently require large forces, special equipment for sound reproduction, extramusical media, and the like. While we might admire composers for daring to impose these requirements, we might sometimes question their motives for doing so. Does the spectacular requirement reflect spectacular vision or an eye for publicity? At a concert I attended recently in the Centre Georges Pompidou, a few players were surrounded by a stage full of electronic equipment. It struck me that this music will have to go forward with a vast amount of electronic baggage (I might add, the same set of baggage). Perhaps technology will have some dirty tricks to play on the music of our century.

We will continue to find loudspeakers a challenge to use in performance, even if the available equipment is not elaborate. We will also discover a thousand compositional ways to compensate for loudspeaker-performer imbalance. And, if we pay some attention to the performance spaces and loudspeaker placement in them, the good compositions will succeed as always.

Notes

1. Max Mathews, "The Computer as a Musical Instrument," *Science* 142 (1963): 553.

2. Henry Brant, "Space as an Essential Aspect of Musical Composition," in *Contemporary Composers on Contemporary Music*, ed. E. Schwarz and B. Childs (New York: Holt, Rinehart, and Winston, 1966), pp. 223–42.

3. H. Wallach, E. B. Newman and M. R. Rosenzweig, "The Precedence Effect in Sound Localization," *American Journal of Psychology* 62 (1949): 315–36.

Bibliography

Appleton, Jon H. "New Role for the Composer." *Music Journal* 27 (March 1969): 14–20.

———. "Live and In Concert: Composer/Performer Views of Real-Time Performance Systems." *Computer Music Journal* 8, no. 1 (Spring 1984): 48–51.

Appleton, Jon H., and Ron C. Perera, eds. *The Development and Practice of Electronic Music.* Englewood Cliffs, N.J.: Prentice-Hall, 1975.

Arveiller, Jacques. "Comments on University Instruction in Computer Music." *Computer Music Journal* 6, no. 2 (Summer 1982): 72–78.

Austin, William W. *Music in the 20th Century.* New York: W. W. Norton, 1966.

Babbitt, Milton. "The Revolution in Sound: Electronic Music." *Music Journal* 18, no. 7 (October 1960): 23–32.

———. "The Synthesis, Perception and Specification of Musical Time." *International Folk Music* 16 (1964): 41–53.

Barrière, Jean-Baptiste. "'Chréode 1': The Pathway to New Music with the Computer." *Contemporary Music Review* 1, pt. 1 (1984): 66–69.

Basart, Ann Phillips. *Serial Music: A Classified Bibliography of Writings on Twelve-Tone and Electronic Music.* Berkeley: University of California Press, 1961.

Bateman, Wayne. *Introduction to Computer Music.* New York: John Wiley and Sons, 1980.

Batticr, Marc and Barry Truax, eds. *Computer Music, Composition Musicale par Ordinateur, Report on an International Project Including a Workshop at Aarhus, Denmark in 1978.* Ottawa: Canadian Commission for UNESCO, 1978.

Beauchamp, James and Heinz von Foerster, eds. *Music by Computers.* New York: John Wiley and Sons, 1969.

Beckwith, John and Udo Kasemets. *The Modern Composer and His World.* Toronto: University of Toronto Press, 1961.

Behrman, David. "The Changing Landscape of Contemporary Music," *Bandwagon* 12, no. 5, (November 1965): 43–46.

Bornoff, Jack, ed. *Music Theatre in a Changing Society.* Paris: UNESCO, 1968.

Brün, Herbert. "Technology and the Composer." *UNESCO Conference on Music and Technology.* June 1970.

Buxton, William. "A Composer's Introduction to Computer Music." *Interface* 6, no. 2 (1977): 57–71.

Cage, John and Lejaren Hiller. "HPSCHD," *Source* 4, no. 2 (July 1968): 10–19.

Ceely, Robert. "Electronic Music Three Ways." *Electronic Music Review* 1 (January 1967): 1–7.

Chadabe, Joel. "Interactive Composing: An Overview." *Computer Music Journal* 8, no. 1 (Spring 1984): 22–27.

Chamberlin, Hal. *Musical Applications of Micro-Processors.* N.J.: Hayden Book Company, 1980.

Ciamaga, Gustav and J. Gabura. "Training of the Composer in New Technological Means." *UNESCO Conference on Music and Technology.* June 1970.

Cohen, David. "Computer-Generated Music." Southeastern Composers League *Newsletter.* December 1966.

"Computer Performances of Music." Reports and discussion: J. K. Randall, Herbert Brün, Ercolino Ferretti, Godfrey Winham, Lejaren Hiller, David Lewin, and Harold Shapiro. American Society of University Composer *Proceedings,* 1966.

Cope, David. *New Music Composition.* New York: Schirmer Books, 1977.

———. *New Directions in Music—1950 to 1970.* 3d Edition. Dubuque Iowa: William C. Brown Company Publishers, 1981.

Davies, Hugh, ed. *International Electronic Music Catalogue.* Cambridge: M.I.T. Press, 1967.

Deutsch, Herbert A. *Synthesis—An Introduction, Theory and Practice of Electronic Music.* New York: Alfred Publishing Company, 1976.

Eaton, John. "The Humanization of Electronic Music." *Music Educators Journal* 55, no. 3 (November 1968): 17–24.

Ehle, Robert C. "The Social World of Electronic Music," *Instrumentalist,* October 1970, 49–57.

Eimert, Herbert. "What is Electronic Music?" *Die Reihe* 1 (1955): 1–10.

Electronic Music in Sweden. Stockholm: Swedish Music Information Center, 1972.

Ernst, David. *The Evolution of Electronic Music.* New York: Schirmer Books, 1977.

Gerzso, Andrew. "Reflections on Répons." *Contemporary Music Review* 1, pt. 1 (1984): 16–22.

Goeyvaerts, Karel. "The Sound Material of Electronic Music," *Die Reihe* 1 (1955): 35–7.

Griffiths, Paul. "Three works by Jonathan Harvey: The Electronic Mirror." *Contemporary Music Review* 1, pt. 1 (1984): 70–76.

Harvey, Jonathan. " 'Mortuos Plango, Vivos Voco': A Realization at IRCAM." *Computer Music Journal* 5, no. 4 (Winter 1981): 22–24.

———. "Reflection after Composition." *Contemporary Music Review* 1, pt. 1 (1984): 23–31.

Heifetz, Robin Julian. "Japanese Analog Electroacoustic Music." *Interface* 9, no. 2 (1980): 71–82.

Heifetz, Robin and Rodney Oakes. "Electro-Acoustic Studios in Los Angeles." *Journal of The Society for Electro-Acoustic Music in the United States, Inc.* 1, no. 1 (April 1986): 9–10.

Hiller, Lejaren and Leonard M. Isaacson. *Experimental Music.* New York: McGraw-Hill, 1959.

Höller, York. "Composition of the Gestalt, or the Making of an Organism." *Contemporary Music Review* 1, pt. 1 (1984): 61–65.

————. "Resonance: Composition Today." *Contemporary Music Review* 1, pt. 1 (1984): 45–48.

Howe, Hubert S., Jr. "A General View of Compositional Procedure in Computer Sound Synthesis." *American Society of University Composers Proceedings,* (1968): 98–108.

————. *Electronic Music Synthesis.* New York: W. W. Norton and Company, 1975.

Jameux, Dominique. "Boulez and the 'Machine': Some Thoughts on the Composer's Use of Various Electro-acoustic Media." *Contemporary Music Review* 1, pt. 1 (1984): 57–60.

Judd, Frederick C. *Electronic Music and Musique Concrète.* England: Neville Spearman, 1961.

————. *Electronics in Music.* England: Neville Spearman, Ltd., 1972.

Kaegi, Werner. *Was ist elektronische Musik?* Basel: Orell Füssli, 1967.

Keane, David. "Computer Music: New Tools for Old Problems." *Humanities Association Review* 30, no. 1–2, (Winter–Spring 1979): 73–87.

————. *Tape Music Composition.* New York: Oxford University Press, 1981.

Koblyakov, Lev. "Jean-Claude Risset—'Songes (1979) (9').'" *Contemporary Music Review* 1, pt. 1 (1984): 49–56.

Koenig, Gottfried M. "The Use of Computer Programmes in Creating Music." *UNESCO Conference on Music and Technology.* June 1970.

————. "Aesthetic Integration of Computer-Composed Scores." *Computer Music Journal* 7, no. 4 (Winter 1983): 27–32.

Kowarski, Lew. "Man-Computer Symbiosis: Fears and Hopes." In Mumford, E. and H. Sackman, eds. *Human Choice and Computers.* Amsterdam Netherlands: North-Holland Publishing Company, 1975.

Ligeti, György. "Metamorphoses of Musical Form." *Die Reihe* 7 (1969): 5–19.

Lincoln, Harry B., ed. *The Computer and Music.* New York: Cornell University Press, 1970.

Lincoln, Harry B. "Uses of the Computer in Music Composition and Research." In *Advances in Computers.* Edited by Morris Rubinoff, vol. 12. 1972.

Lucier, Alvin. "The Making of 'North American Time Capsule 1967.'" *Electronic Music Review* 5 (January 1968): 30–36.

Luening, Otto. "Some Random Remarks About Electronic Music." *Journal of Music Theory* 8, no. 1 (1964): 89–98.

Machover, Tod. "A view of music at IRCAM." *Contemporary Music Review* 1, pt. 1 (1984): 1–8.

————. "Computer Music with and without Instruments." *Contemporary Music Review* 1, pt. 1 (1984): 9–15.

McNabb, Michael. "'Dreamsong': The Composition." *Computer Music Journal* 5, no. 4 (Winter 1981): 36–53.

Melby, Carol. *Computer Music Compositions of the United States 1976.* Virginia: Theodore Front, 1976.

"Mixed-Media Composition." Panel discussion: Ross Lee Finney, George Cacciopo, Edwin London, and Salvatore Martirano. American Society of University Composers *Proceedings* (1968): 123–145.

Mumma, Gordon. "Alvin Lucier's 'Music for Solo Performer 1965.'" *Source* 1, no. 2 (July 1967): 32–35.

Norton, Richard. "The Vision of Morton Subotnick." *Music Journal* 28 (January 1970): 14–21.

Oliveros, Pauline. "Some Sound Observations." *Source* 2, no. 1 (January 1968): 77–79.

———. "Tape Delay Techniques for Electronic Music Composition." *The Composer* 1, no. 3 (December 1969): 135–142.

Pellegrino, Ronald. *The Electronic Arts of Sound and Light.* New York: Van Nostrand Reinhold, 1983.

Pousseur, Henri. "Formal Elements in a New Compositional Material." *Die Reihe* 1 (1955): 30–4.

Powell, Mel. "Electronic Music and Musical Newness." *The American Scholar* 35, no. 2, (Spring 1966): 46–60.

Pulfer, J. K. "Computer Aid for Musical Composers," *Bulletin of Radio and Electrical Engineering Division* 20, no. 2 (1970): 44–48.

Randall, J. K. "Electronic Music and Musical Tradition." *Music Educators Journal* 55, no. 3 (November 1968): 25–35.

"Recent Developments in Electronic Music." Panel discussion: Hubert S. Howe, Jr., David Cohen, Emmanuel Ghent, Max Matthews, and Robert Moog. American Society of University Composers *Proceedings* (1969): 7–37.

Roads, Curtis and John Strawn, eds. *Foundations of Computer Music.* Cambridge: M.I.T. Press, 1985.

Salzman, Eric. *Twentieth Century Music—An Introduction.* Englewood Cliffs, N.J.: Prentice-Hall, 1967.

Schafer, R. Murray. *Ear Cleaning.* Toronto, Ontario: BMI Canada, 1967.

Schaeffer, Pierre. *Traité des objets musicaux.* Paris: Editions du Seuil, 1966.

———. "La musique et les ordinateurs." *UNESCO Conference on Music and Technology,* June 1970.

Schrader, Barry. *Introduction to Electro-Acoustic Music.* Englewood Cliffs, N.J.: Prentice-Hall, 1982.

Schwartz, Elliot. "Elevator Music." *The Composer* 2, no. 2 (September 1970): 16–23.

———. *Electronic Music: A Listener's Guide.* Revised Edition. New York: Praeger Publishers, 1975.

Schwartz, Elliot and Barney Childs, eds. *Contemporary Composers on Contemporary Music.* New York: Holt, Rinehart and Winston, 1967.

Slonimsky, Nicolas. *Music Since 1900.* 4th Edition. New York: Charles Scribner's Sons, 1971.

Smith-Brindle, Reginald. "The Lunatic Fringe: 1. Concrete Music. 2. Electronic Music. 3. Computation Composition." *The Musical Times* 97 (1956): 246.

Stockhausen, Karlheinz. "Electronic and Instrumental Music." *Die Reihe* 5 (1959): 59–67.

Strange, Allen. "Tape Piece." *The Composer* 2, no. 1 (June 1970): 1–12.

Stroppa, Marco. "The Analysis of Electronic Music." *Contemporary Music Review* 1, pt. 1 (1984): 32–44.

Stuckenschmidt, H. H. "Contemporary Techniques in Music." *The Musical Quarterly* 49, no. 1 (January 1963): 1–16.

———. *Twentieth Century Music*. Translated by Richard Deveson, New York: McGraw-Hill, 1969.

Subotnick, Morton. "Extending the Stuff Music Is Made Of." *Music Educators Journal* 55, no. 3 (November 1968): 1–16.

———. "The Synthesizer: Is It the Ultimate Musical Weapon?" *Recording Engineer/Producer* 1, no. 1 (April–May 1970): 12–16.

Truax, Barry. "The Computer Composition—Sound Synthesis Programs POD4, POD5, and POD6." *Sonological Reports* 2 (1973): 15–31.

———. "A Communicational Approach to Computer Sound Programs." *Journal of Music Theory* 20, no. 2 (1976): 227–300.

Trythall, Gilbert. *Principles and Practice of Electronic Music*. New York: Grosset and Dunlap, 1973.

Vercoe, Barry L. "Electronic Sounds and the Sensitive Performer." *Music Educators Journal,* 55, no. 3 (November 1968): 36–41.

———. "Man-Computer Interaction in Creative Applications." Typescript. 1975.

Wells, Thomas and Eric S. Vogel, eds. *The Techniques of Electronic Music*. New York: Schirmer Books, 1981.

Whipple, H. "Beasts and Butterflies: Morton Subotnick's Ghost Scores." *The Musical Quarterly* 69, no. 3 (Summer 1983): 425–41.

Yates, Peter. *Twentieth-Century Music*. New York: Pantheon Books, 1967.

Zimmermann, Walter, ed. *Desert Plants*. Canada: A.R.C. Publications, 1976.

Recordings

Robert Aitken	"Noesis," Folkways FMS 33436.
Ruth Anderson	"I Come out of Your Sleep," Opus One 63.
Jon H. Appleton	"Appleton Syntonic," Flying Dutchman FDS 103. "Menagerie," Flying Dutchman FDS 103. "The World Music Theatre of Jon Appleton," Folkways FTS 33437. "Georganna's Farewell," Folkways FTS 33442. "In deserto," Folkways FTS 33445. "Synthropia," Folkways FTS 33445. "The Sydsing Camklang," Folkways FTS 33445. "Zoetrope," Folkways FTS 33445. "Mussems Sang," Folkways FTS 33445. "The Sweet Dream of Miss Pamela Beach," Folkways FTS 37461. "Sashasonjon," Folkways FTS 37461. "Kapincamaranci," Folkways FTS 37461. "Nukuoro," Folkways FTS 37461.

Bülent Arel	"Electronic Music No. 1," CRI S-356.
	"Music for a Sacred Service," CRI S-356.
	"Prelude and Postlude," CRI S-356.
	"Stereo Electronic Music No. 2," Finnadar FIN 9010 (Q).
	"Mimiana I: Flux," Finnadar FIN 9020.
	"Mimiana II: Frieze," Finnadar FIN 9020.
	"Mimiana III: Six and Seven," Finnadar FIN 9020.
	"Fragment," Orpheum SN-3.
Robert Ashley	"The Wolfman," ESP-DISK S-1009.
	"Untitled Mixes," ESP-DISK S-1009.
	"Automatic Writing," Lovely VR-1002.
	"Sonata," Lovely VR-1062.
	"Coo Coo Music Word Fire," Lovely VR-4908.
	"She Was a Visitor," Odyssey 32160156.
Larry Austin	"Canadian Coastlines," Folkways FTS 37475.
	"Catalogo Voce," Irida IR-0022.
	"Maroon Bells," Irida IR-0022.
	"Quadrants: Event/Complex No. 1," Irida IR-0022.
	"Second Fantasy on Ives' Universe Symphony—The Heavens," Irida IR-0022.
	"Caritas," Source SR 17 39194.
Milton Babbitt	"Composition for Synthesizer," Columbia MS-6566.
	"Ensembles for Synthesizer," Columbia MS-7051.
	"Vision and Prayer," CRI 268.
Henk Badings	"Capriccio for Violin and Two Sound Tracks," Epic BC 1118.
	"Evolutionen," Epic BC 1118.
	"Genese," Epic BC 1118.
Jürgen Bäuninger	"The Tam Tam Tape," Ornament Edition Neue Musik CH-7.921.

François Bayle	"Vapeur," BAM BOITE À MUSIQUE LD 072.
	"Espaces inhabitables," INA, Collection GRM, Serie Gramme G101 BA (Paris).
	"Tremblement de terre très doux," INA, Collection GRM, Serie Gramme G101 BA.
	"Trois rêves d'oiseau," INA, Collection GRM, Serie Gramme G101 BA.
	"Andromède," Musique pour l'Image MPI/LP-105.
	"Titan," Musique pour l'Image MPI/LP-105.
David Behrman	"Figure in a Clearing," Lovely LML-1041.
	"On the Other Ocean," Lovely LML-1041.
Luciano Berio	"Perspectives," Compagnia Generale del Disco ESZ3 (Milan).
	"Momenti," Mercury SR2-9123.
	"Thema—Omaggio a Joyce," Turnabout TV-34177.
Karl-Birger Blomdahl	"Aniara: Suite of Electronic Interludes," Columbia MS-7176.
Lars-Gunnar Bodin	"Bilder," Folkways 33442.
	"For Jon (Fragments of a Time to Come)," Folkways 33443.
Benjamin Boretz	"Group Variations for Computer," CRI SD-300.
André Boucourechliev	"Texte I, Mercury SR2-9123.
Robert Boyer	"Illusions I," Redwood ES-10.
Jean-Louis Brau	"Instrumentation verbale," Achele JLB1 (Paris).
Earle Brown	"Octet I," CRI SD-330.
	"Times Five," CRI SD-330.

Herbert Brün:

"Anepigraphe," Amadeus 106.
"Klänge Unterwegs (Wayfaring Sounds)," Amadeus 106.
"A Mere Ripple," Lingua Press.
"Dust," Lingua Press.
"I toLD You so!" Lingua Press.
"More Dust," Lingua Press.
"U-TURN-TO," Lingua Press.
"Dustiny," Non-Sequitur Records 301056.
"Piece of Prose," Non-Sequitur Records 301057.
"Sonoriferous Loops," Non Sequitur Records 301057.
"Futility 1964," Non-Sequitur Records 301058.
"Non Sequitur VI," Non-Sequitur Records 301058.

Ton Bruynèl

"Phases," Donemus CV 8003 (Amsterdam).
"Serène," Donemus CV 8003.
"Soft Song," Donemus CV 8003.
"Toccare," Donemus CV 8003.
"Translucent II," Donemus CV 8003.
"Collage Resonance II," Europese Fonoclub EFC 2501 (Amsterdam).
"Reflexen," Europese Fonoclub EFC 2501.
"Reliëf," Europese Fonoclub EFC 2501.

Harold Budd

"Coeur d'Orr," Advance 16.
"Oak of Golden Dreams," Advance 16.

John Cage

"Feed," Columbia MS 7139.
"Fontana Mix," Columbia MS 7139.
"Radio Music," Cramp CRSLP 6101.
"Cartridge Music," Deutsche Grammophon DGG 137009.
"Variations IV," Everest SDBR 3132.
"Solos for Voice 2," Odyssey 32160156.
"Aria, with Fontana Mix," Time 58003.

John Cage and Lejaren Hiller	"HPSCHD, for Harpsichords and Computer-Generated Sound Tapes," Nonesuch H-71224.
Canadian Electronic Ensemble	"Chaconne à son gout," Centredisc 1.
Robert Ceely	"Stratti and Vonce," Beep 1001. "Elegia," CRI S-328. "Mitsyn," CRI S-328.
John Celona	"Music in Circular Motions," Folkways FTS 37475.
Sergio Cervetti	"Aria Suspendida," CRI S-359.
Joel Chadabe	"Echoes," Folkways 33904. "Rhythms," Lovely VR-1301. "Settings for Spirituals," Lovely VR-1302. "Solo," Lovely VR-1302. "Street Scene," Opus One 16. "Ideas of Movement at Bolton Landing," Opus One 17.
David Cope	"Visions: Music for Orchestra, 2 Pianos, and Computer-Generated Tape," Folkways 33452. "Navajo Dedications," Folkways 33869.
Conrad Cummings	"Beast Songs," CRI S-487.
Alvin Curran	"Songs and Views from the Magnetic Garden," Ananda No. 1 (Italy). "Fiori Chiari, Fiori Oscuri," Ananda No. 4.
James Dashow	"Conditional Assemblies," Edi-Pan PRC S 20-12 (Italy). "Effetti Collaterali," Edi-Pan PRC S 20-12. "Partial Distances," Edi-Pan PRC S 20-12.

Mario Davidovsky	"Electronic Study No. 1," Columbia MS 6566.
	"Synchronism No. 1," CRI S-204.
	"Synchronism No. 2," CRI S-204.
	"Synchronism No. 3," CRI S-204.
	"Synchronism No. 5," CRI S-268.
	"Electronic Study No. 2," CRI S-356.
	"Electronic Study No. 3," Finnadar FIN 9010 (Q).
Alfredo del Monaco	"Electronic Study No. 2," CRI S-328.
	"Metagrama," CRI S-328.
Tod Dockstader	"Eight Electronic Pieces," Folkways FM 3434.
	"Apocalypse," Owl ORLP 6.
	"Luna Park," Owl ORLP 6.
	"Traveling Music," Owl ORLP 6.
	"Drone," Owl ORLP 7.
	"Water Music," Owl ORLP 7.
	"Quatermass," Owl ORLP 8.
Tod Dockstader and James Reichert	"Omniphony I," Owl ORLP 11.
Charles Dodge	"Extensions," CRI S-300.
	"Folia," CRI S-300.
	"In Celebration," CRI S-348.
	"Speech Songs," CRI S-348.
	"The Story of Our Lives," CRI S-348.
	"Cascando," CRI S-454.
	"Any Resemblance is Purely Coincidental," Folkways FTS 37475.
	"Changes," Nonesuch H-71245.
	"Earth's Magnetic Field," Nonesuch H-71250.
Franco Donatoni	"Quartetto III," Compagnia Generale del Disco ESZ3.
Jacob Druckman	"Animus II," CRI S-255.
	"Animus I," Turnabout TV-34177.
László Dubrovay	"Oscillation No. 1," SLPX 12030 (Hungary).
	"Oscillation No. 2," SLPX 12030.
	"Oscillation No. 3," SLPX 12030.

John Duesenberry	"Four Movements," Opus One 60. "Moduletone," Opus One 60. "Phrase," Opus One 60. "3 Variations, 2 Interludes," Opus One 60.
François Dufrène and Jean Baronnet	"U 47," Mercury SR2-9123.
John Eaton	"Blind Man's Cry," CRI S-296. "Mass," CRI S-296.
Herbert Eimert	"Etüde über Tongemische," DGG LP 16132. "Fünf Stücke," DGG LP 16132. "Glockenspiel," DGG LP 16132. "Sélection I," Mercury SD2–9123.
Simon Emmerson	"Ophelia's Dream II," Hyperion A 66060 (Great Britain).
Giuseppe G. Englert	"Juralpyroc," Gallo 30-380 (Switzerland).
Donald Erb	"In No Strange Land," Nonesuch H-71223. "Reconnaissance," Nonesuch H-71223.
Richard Feliciano	"Chod," CRI S-349.
Brian Fennelly	"Evanescences," CRI S-322.
Luc Ferrari	"Etude aux accidents," BAM BOITE À MUSIQUE EX 241. "Etude aux sons tendus," BAM BOITE À MUSIQUE EX 242. "Tautologos II," BAM BOITE À MUSIQUE LD 071. "Tautologos II," BAM BOITE À MUSIQUE LD 072. "Presque rien n° 2," INA/GRM 9 104 FR Serie Gramme. "Promenade symphonique à travers un paysage musical (Algérie n° 4)," INA/GRM 9 104 FE, Serie Gramme. "Visage V," Limelight LS-86047. "Tête et queue du dragon," Philips 835 487 AY.

Kenneth Gaburo	"For Harry," Heliodor HS-25047.
	"Lemon Drops," Heliodor HS-25047.
	"Antiphony III (Pearl-White Moments)," Nonesuch H-71199.
	"Antiphony IV (Poised)," Nonesuch H 71199.
	"Exit Music I: The Wasting of Lucrecetzia," Nonesuch H-71199.
	"Exit Music II: Fat Millie's Lament," Nonesuch H-71199.
Emmanuel Ghent	"Brazen," Tulsa TS78-208.
Lucien Goethals	"Cellotape," Alpha 5.066-5 (Belgium).
	"Meliorbis," IPEM 10 (Belgium).
	"Studie I," IPEM 10.
	"Studie VIIb," IPEM 10.
Victor Grauer	"Inferno," Folkways FMS 33436.
Jan Greenwald	"Durations 2," CRI S-443.
Joel Gressel	"Crossings," CRI S-393.
	"P-Vibes: 3 Canons," CRI S-393.
	"Points in Time," Odyssey Y-34139.
Ragnar Grippe	"Musique douze," CRI S-364.
	"Ten Temperaments," Grammofon AB BIS LP-241 (Sweden).
Bengt Hambraeus	"Constellations II," Limelight LS-86052.
	"Interferences," Limelight LS-86052.
Charles Hamm	"Canto 1963," Heliodor HS-25047.
Kevin Hanlon	"Variations," CRI S-431.
	"Through to the End of the Tunnel," Folkways FPX 6050.
Stanley Haynes	"Prisms," Folkways FTS 37475.

Robin Julian Heifetz	"Spectre," Atelier Créatif de Musique Électro-Acoustique (ACME) (Belgium).
	"Wanderer," ACME.
	"A Clear and Present Danger," Folkways FSS 33787.
	"Flykt," Orion ORS 80366.
	"För Anders Lundberg: Mardröm 29 30 10," Orion ORS 80366.
	"Susurrus," Orion ORS 80366.
	"Wasteland," Orion ORS 80366.
William Hellermann	"EK-Stasis," CRI S-299.
Pierre Henry	"Orphée," Critère CRD 140 (Paris).
	"L'occident est bleu—L'an 56," Disco-livre (Paris).
	"Batterie fugace," Ducretet-Thomson 320 C 100 (Paris).
	"Concerto des Ambiguïtés (Final)," Ducretet-Thomson 320 C 100.
	"Le voile d'Orphée," Ducretet-Thomson 320 C 100.
	"Musique sans titre (mouvements 5 et 6)," Ducretet-Thomson 320 C 100.
	"Tam-Tam III," Ducretet-Thomson 320 C 100.
	"Antiphonie," Ducretet-Thomson 320 C 102.
	"Astrologie," Ducretet-Thomson 320 C 102.
	"Tam-Tam IV," Ducretet-Thomson 320 C 102.
	"Vocalises," Ducretet-Thomson 320 C 102.
	"Spatiodynamisme I," Edition du Griffon (Switzerland).
	"Spatiodynamisme II," Edition du Griffon.
	"Le Voyage," Limelight LS-86049.
	"Investigations: Entité," Mercury SR2-9123.
	"Entité," Philips J804.

Pierre Henry and Pierre Schaeffer	"Bidule en ut," Ducretet-Thomson 320 C 100. "Symphonie pour un homme seul," Ducretet-Thomson 320 C 102.
Hans Werner Henze	"Tristan," DGG 2530 834.
Lejaren Hiller	"Malta," Capra 1206. "A Portfolio for Diverse Performers and Tape," CRI S-438. "Algorithms I (Version I)," DGG 2543-005. "Algorithms II (Version IV)," DGG 2543-005. "Machine Music," Heliodor HS-25074. "Avalanche," Heliodor HS-2549006. "Computer Music," Heliodor HS-2549006. "Suite for Two Pianos and Tape," He- liodor HS-2549006.
Lejaren Hiller and Robert Baker	"Computer Cantata," CRI S-310.
Lejaren Hiller and Leonard M. Issaacson	"Illiac Suite," Heliodor HS-25053.
Richard Hoffmann	"In Memoriam Patris," CRI S-393.
Reed Holms	"Around the Waves," Advance FGR-6. "Nova," Folkways FPX 6050. "Moiré," Folkways FSS 37465.
Hubert S. Howe	"Canons 4," Opus One 47. "Third Study in Timbre," Opus One 47.
Joseph Hudson	"Sonare," CRI S-382.
Jerry Hunt	"Cantegral Segments," Irida IR-0032.
Toshi Ichiyanagi	"Music for Tinguely," Minami Gallery (Tokyo). "Life Music," Nippon Victor SJV 1501 (Tokyo). "Extended Voices," Odyssey 32160156.
Jean Eichelberger Ivey	"Hera, Hung from the Sky," CRI S-325. "Pinball," Folkways FMS 33436.

Bengt Emil Johnson	"Disappearances," CRI S-364.
Mauricio Kagel	"Transition I," Mercury SR2-9123.
Erhard Karkoshka	"Dialog," Ornament Edition Neue Musik CH-7.921.
David Keane	"Electronikus Mozaik," Cambridge Street Records CSR 8502 (Canada).
	"La Aurora Estrellada," Cambridge Street Records CSR 8502.
	"La cascade enchantée," Cambridge Street Records, CSR 8502.
	"Elegy," Music Gallery Editions MGE 29.
	"Evening Song," Music Gallery Editions MGE 29.
	"In Memoriam: Hugh LeCaine," Music Gallery Editions MGE 29.
	"Lyra," Music Gallery Editions MGE 29.
Gershon Kingsley and Jean-Jacques Perrey	"The In Sound from Way Out," Vanguard VSD 79222.
Gottfried Michael Koenig	"Klangfiguren II," DGG LP 16134.
Karl Korte	"The Whistling Wind," Folkways FSS 37465.
	"Remembrances," Nonesuch H-71289.
Witold Kotónski	"Etiuda na jedno uderzenie w talerz," MUZA 200 (W 680) (Warsaw).
	"Mikrostruktury," MUZA 211 (W 873/874).
Leo Kraft	"Dialogues for Flute and Tape," CRI S-292.
Jonathan D. Kramer	"Renascence," Grenadilla 1017.
Arthur Krieger	"Dance for Sarah," CRI S-483.
	"Theme and Variations," CRI S-483.
	"Short Piece," Odyssey Y-34139.
Meyer Kupferman	"Superflute," Nonesuch H-71289.
Joan LaBarbara	"Cathing," Chi-Sound CHI 196.
	"Thunder," Chi-Sound CHI 196.
Paul Lansky	"Mild und Leise," Odyssey Y-34139.
Hugh LeCaine	"Dripsody," Folkways FMS 33436.

Peter Tod Lewis	"Gestes," CRI S-324. "Signs and Circuits," CRI S-392.
Györgi Ligeti	"Artikulation," Philips J804.
Annea Lockwood	"World Rhythms," 1750 Arch 1765. "Tiger Balm," Opus One 70.
Alvin Lucier	"Long Thin Wire Installation," Lovely VR-1001/2. "I Am Sitting in a Room," Lovely VR-1013. "North American Time Capsule 1967," Odyssey 32160156.
Otto Luening	"Gargoyles," Columbia MS 6566. "Synthesis for Orchestra and Electronic Sound," CRI S-219. "In the Beginning (from Theatre Piece No. 2)," CRI S-268. "Fantasy in Space," Desto 6466. "Invention," Desto 6466. "Legend," Desto 6466. "Low Speed," Desto 6466. "Lyric Speed," Desto 6466. "Moonlight," Desto 6466.
Otto Luening and Vladimir Ussachevsky	"A Poem in Cycles and Bells," CRI S-112. "Suite from King Lear," CRI S-112. "Concerted Piece," CRI S-227. "Incantation," Desto 6466. "Rhapsodic Variations," Louisville LOU 545-5.
Bruno Maderna	"Musica su due dimensioni (II)," Compagnia Generale del Disco ESZ3. "Continuo," Mercury SR2-9123.
Ivo Malec	"Reflets," BAM BOITE À MUSIQUE LD 072.
Salvatore Martirano	"Underworld," Heliodor HS-25047. "L's G A," Polydor Stereo 24-5001.

Max Mathews	"Numerology," Decca DL 79103. "The Second Law," Decca DL 71903. "Cyclic Study," Gravesaner Blätter EP ML 372 (Mainz). "Masquerades," Gravesaner Blätter EP ML 372. "Pergolesi Development," Gravesaner Blätter EP ML 372. "Substitution Study," Gravesaner Blätter EP ML 372.
William Matthews	"Field Guide," CRI S-375. "Aurora, A Waltz," CRI S-483.
Richard Maxfield	"Amazing Grace," Advance S-8. "Bacchanale," Advance S-8. "Pastoral Symphony," Advance S-8. "Night Music," Odyssey 32160160.
Barton McLean	"Dimensions I," Advance FGR-25. "Spirals," CRI S-335. "Dimensions III," CRI S-431. "Dimensions IV," CRI S-431. "Heavy Music for Four Crowbars," Folkways FPX 6050. "Song of the Nahuatl," Folkways FTS 33450. "Etunytude," Folkways FSS 37465. "The Last Ten Minutes," Folkways FSS 37465. "Dimensions II," Orion ORS 75192. "Genesis," Orion ORS 75192. "The Sorcerer Revisited," Orion ORS 75192.
Priscilla McLean	"Dance of Dawn," CRI S-335. "Invisible Chariots," Folkways FTS 33450.
Randall McClelland	"Music of the Spheres and Processional," CRI S-382. "Distant Voices," Opus One 17. "Genesis," Opus One 24. "Interruptions," Opus One 24.

Michael McNabb	"Dreamsong," 1750 Arch S-1800. "Illusoria," 1750 Arch S-1800. "Love in the Asylum," 1750 Arch S-1800. "Mad as Birds," 1750 Arch S-1800. "Orbital Vicw," 1750 Arch S-1800.
John Melby	"Chor der Steine," Advance FGR-6. "91 Plus 5," CRI S-310. "Two Stevens Songs," CRI S-364. "Forandrer: 7 Variations for Digital Computer," UAS 869-62984.
Roger Meyers	"After the Pond," Opus One 63.
Ilhan Mimaroğlu	"Wings of the Delirious Demon," Finnadar FIN 9001. "For Dubuffet's Coucou Bazaar," Finnadar FIN 9003. "Agony," Finnadar FIN 9012. "Bowery Bum," Finnadar FIN 9012. "8 Preludes for Magnetic Tape," Finnadar FIN 9012. "Intermezzo," Finnadar FIN 9012. "Le Tombeau d'Edgar Poe," Finnadar FIN 9012. "Tract," Folkways 33441. "To Kill a Sunrise," Folkways 33951 (Q). "Six Preludes for Magnetic Tape," Turnabout TV-34177.
Dexter Morrill	"Studies for Trumpet and Computer," Golden Crest RE-7068. "Six Dark Questions," Redwood ES-10. "Fantasy Quintet," Redwood ES-13. "No," Redwood ES-13.
Lawrence Moss	"Evocation and Song," Opus One 16.

Gordon Mumma	"Peasant Boy," ESP-DISK S-1009. "Cybersonic Cantilevers," Folkways 33904. "Megaton for William Burroughs," Lovely LML/VR-1091. "Music from the Venezia Space Theater," Lovely LML/VR-1091. "The Dresden Interleaf 13 February 1945," Lovely LML/VR-1091. "Mesa for Cybersonic Bandoneon," Odyssey 32160158.
Vaclav Nelhybel	"Outer Space Music," Folkways 33440.
David Olan	"Compositions for Clarinet and Tape," CRI S-419.
Pauline Oliveros	"I of IV," Odyssey 32160160. "Bye Bye Butterfly," 1750 Arch 1765.
Bernard Parmegiani	"De Natura Sonorum," INA/Collection GRM, AM 714.01.
Bruce Pennycook	"Speeches for Dr. Frankenstein," Folkways FTS 37475. "If Carillons Grew Wings," Redwood ES-10.
Ronald Perera	"Alternate Routes," CRI S-364. "Three Poems of Gunter Grass," CRI S-420.
Tracy Lind Peterson	"Voices," Tulsa TS78-208.
Russell Pinkston	"Emergence," Folkways 33442.
Zoltán Pongrácz	"Phonothèse," DGG 137011. "In Praise of Folly," Qualiton SLPX 12433. "Madrigal, On Petrach's Sonnet LXI," Qualiton SLPX 12433. "144 Sounds," Qualiton SLPX 12433. "Sesquialtera," Qualiton SLPX 12433.
Henri Pousseur	"Trois visages de Liège," Columbia MS-7051. "Scambi (Echanges)," Mercury SR2-9123. "Rimes pour différentes sources sonores," Victrola VICS-1239.

Mel Powell	"Improvisation," CRI S-227. "Second Electronic Setting," CRI S-227. "2 Prayer Settings," CRI S-227.
J.K. Randall	"Music for the Film 'Eakins,'" CRI S-328. "Mudgett: Monologues by a Mass Murderer," Nonesuch H-71245. "Quartersines," Nonesuch H-71245. "Quartets in Pairs," Nonesuch H-71245.
Michel Redolfi	"Immersion," INA/Collection GRM 3D 833.12. "Pacific Tubular Waves," INA/Collection GRM 3D 833.12.
Phillip Rehfeldt	"Music for Clarinet and Tape," Grenadilla 1005.
Steve Reich	"Come Out," Odyssey 32160160.
Roger Reynolds	"Ping," CRI S-285. "Traces," CRI S-285.
Jean-Claude Risset	"Inharmonic Soundscapes," Tulsa TS78-208.
John Donald Robb	"Rhythmania," Folkways 33435. "Collage," Folkways FMS 33436. "From Razor Blades to Moog," Folkways 33438. "Toccata," Opus One 42.
David Rosenboom and Donald Buchla	"And Out Come The Night Bars," 1750 Arch S-1774. "How Much Better if Plymouth Rock Had Landed on the Pilgrims," 1750 Arch S-1774.
Eric Ross	"Electronic Etudes," Doria 103.
Howard Rovics	"Piece for Cello, Piano, and Electronic Tape," CRI S-392.
Andrew Rudin	"Tragoedia, A Composition in 4 Movements for Electronic Music Synthesizer," Nonesuch H-71198.

Eric Salzman	"Helix," Finnadar FIN 9005 (Q). "Larynx Music," Finnadar FIN 9005 (Q). "Queens Collage," Finnadar FIN 9005 (Q). "Wiretap," Finnadar FIN 9005 (Q).
Pierre Schaeffer	"Etude aux allures," BAM BOITE À MUSIQUE EX 241. "Etude aux sons animés," BAM BOITE À MUSIQUE EX 242. "Etude aux chemins de fer," Ducretet-Thomson 320 C 100. "Etude aux piano II, dite Etude noire," Ducretet-Thomson 320 C 100. "Etude aux tourniquets," Ducretet-Thomson 320 C 100. "Etude pathétique, dite Etude aux-casseroles," Ducretet-Thomson 320 C 100. "Variations sur une flûte mexicaine," Ducretet-Thomson 320 C 100. "L'Oiseau RAI," Ducretet-Thomson 320 C 102. "Etude aux objets," Philips 835 487 AY.
Barry Schrader	"Trinity," Opus One 93.
Elliott Schwartz	"Extended Piano," Folkways FSS 33431. "Grand Concerto," Folkways FSS 33431. "Mirrors," Folkways FSS 33431. "Music for Prince Albert," Folkways FSS 33431. "Extended Oboe," Organic Oboe O.O. #1.
Daria Semegen	"Spectra (Electronic Composition No. 2)," CRI S-433. "Arc for Dancers," Finnadar FIN 9020. "Electronic Composition No. 1," Odyssey Y-34139.
Alice Shields	"The Transformation of Ani," CRI S-268.

Denis Smalley	"Pneuma," Hyperion A 66060. "Chanson de geste," University of East Anglia UEA 81063 (Great Britain). "Pentes," University of East Anglia UEA 81063. "The Pulses of Time," University of East Anglia UEA 81063.
Pril Smiley	"Kolyosa," CRI S-268. "Eclipse," Finnadar FIN 9010 (Q).
Michael Snow	"Music for Piano, Whistling, Microphone, and Tape Recorder," Chatham Square 1009/10.
Laurie Spiegel	"Appalachian Grove," 1750 Arch 1765.
Karlheinz Stockhausen	"Mikrophonie I," Columbia MS-7355. "Mikrophonie II," Columbia MS-7355. "Studie I," DGG 16133. "Studie II, DGG 16133. "Mixture," DGG 137012. "Telemusik," DGG 137012. "Gesang der Jünglinge," DGG 138811. "Kontakte," DGG 138811. "Opus 1970," DGG 139461 SLPM. "Anthems for Electronic and Concrete Sounds," DGG 2707039. "Hymnen," DGG 2707039. "Spiral," Organic Oboe O.O. #1.
William Strickland	"Electronic Visit to the Zoo," Spectrum 118. "Sound Hypnosis," Spectrum 118.
Morton Subotnick	"Sidewinder," Columbia M-30683. "4 Butterflies," Columbia M-32741. "Silver Apples of the Moon," Nonesuch H-71174. "The Wild Bull," Nonesuch H-71208. "Until Spring," Odyssey Y-34158.
Timothy Sullivan	"Numbers, Names," Redwood ES-10.
Toru Takemitsu	"Vocalism Ai," Nippon Victor SJV 1503-6. "Water Music," Nippon Victor SJV 1503-6.

Jack Tamul   "Electro/Acoustic," Spectrum 134.

Elias Tanenbaum   "Contradictions," CRI S-483.
                         "Blue Fantasy," Desto 7130.
                         "Contrasts," Desto 7130.
                         "For the 'Bird,'" Desto 7130.
                         "Movements," Desto 7130.

Richard Teitelbaum   "Blends," Lumina L005.
                         "Digital Piano Music," Lumina L005.

Diane Thome   "Anais," CRI S-437.
                         "Los Nombres," Tulsa TS78-208.

George Todd   "Satan's Sermon," CRI S-443.
                         "Emergence," Opus One 93.
                         "Voicemask," Opus One 93.

Yuzo Toyama   "Aoi-no-Ue," Folkways FW 8881.
                         "Waka," Folkways FW 8881.

Barry Truax   "Sonic Landscapes," Melbourne SMLP
                             4033 (Canada).

Richard Trythall   "Omaggio a Jerry Lee Lewis," CRI
                             S-382.
                         "Variations on a Theme by Franz
                             Joseph Haydn," CRI S-382.

David Tudor   "Rainforest IV," Editions Block 1.

Vladimir Ussachevsky	"Creation: Prologue," Columbia MS-6566.
	"Of Wood and Brass," CRI S-277.
	"Wireless Fantasy," CRI S-227.
	"Computer Piece No. 1," CRI S-268.
	"2 Sketches," CRI S-268.
	"Three Scenes from the Creation," CRI S-296.
	"Linear Contrasts," CRI S-356.
	"Metamorphosis," CRI S-356.
	"Sonic Contours," Desto 6466.
	"Piece for Tape Recorder," Finnadar FIN 9010 (Q).
	"Transposition, Reverberation, Experiment, Composition," Folkways FX 6160.
	"Underwater Valse," Folkways FX 6160.
	"Conflict," Folkways 33904.
	"Improvisation No. 4711," Orpheum SN-3.
Edgard Varèse	"Poème électronique," Columbia MS-6146.
	"Déserts," CRI S-268.
Barry Vercoe	"Synapse for Viola and Computer," CRI S-393.
	"Synthesism," Nonesuch H-71245.
Reynold Weidenaar	"The Tinsel Chicken Coop Wiener," Advance FGR-6.
Thomas Wells	"11.2.72, Electric Music," CRI S-443.
David Wessel	"Antony," Tulsa TS78-208.
Charles Whittenberg	"Electronic Study No. 2," Advance FGR-1.
Olly Wilson	"Echoes," CRI S-367.
	"Sometimes," CRI S-370.
Godfrey Winham	"N P (2 Pieces for Computer-Synthesized Sound)," CRI S-393.
Trevor Wishart	"Anticredos," Hyperion A 66060.
Charles Wuorinen	"Time's Enconium," Nonesuch H-71225.

Iannis Xenakis	"Diamorphoses," BAM BOITE À MUSIQUE EX 242.
	"Bohor I," Nonesuch H-71246.
	"Concret P-H II," Nonesuch H-71246.
	"Diamorphoses II," Nonesuch H-71246.
	"Orient-Occident III," Nonesuch H-71246.
	"Analogique A + B," Philips 835 487 AY.
	"Concret P-H," Philips 835 487 AY.
	"Atrées," Voix de son maître CVC-2086 (France).
	"Morisma-Amorisma," Voix de son maître CVC-2086.
	"ST/4-1, 080262," Voix de son maître CVC-2086.
Ramon Zupko	"Fluxus I," CRI S-375.
Menachem Zur	"Horizons," Folkways FSS 33878.
	"Chants," Odyssey Y-34139.

Contributors

Jon H. Appleton attended Reed College, where he received the B.A. in 1961, and the University of Oregon, where he received the M.A. in 1965. While at the University of Oregon he began composing electronic music, an interest that led to further study at the Columbia-Princeton Center for Electronic Music, principally under Vladimir Ussachevsky, Mario Davidovsky, and William J. Mitchell. He taught for a year at Oakland University in Rochester, Michigan, before joining the faculty of Dartmouth College in 1967, where he founded and directed the Bregman Electronic Music Studio and in 1979 received an endowed chair. Since 1968 Professor Appleton has worked periodically in Sweden, and in 1976 he directed the Stiftelsen EMS Stockholm. In 1973 in Tonga and in 1979 in Ponape and Truk he took part in projects to record and broadcast traditional Polynesian and Micronesian musics. He received Guggenheim and Fulbright fellowships in 1970 and two National Endowment for the Arts awards in 1976. In writings for popular and scholarly publications he has dealt with the social role, aesthetics, theory, and technology of electronic music, and with Ronald Perera has edited *The Development and Practice of Electronic Music* in 1975.

In the 1970s, concerned that electronic music was functioning primarily as a "studio" rather than a "performing" art, Professor Appleton collaborated with engineer Sydney Alonso and software specialist Cameron Jones to develop the Synclavier, a polyphonic digital synthesizer that can be used for live performance: the first such instrument to utilize microcomputers and the first to be manufactured commercially.

Herbert Brün was born in 1918 in Berlin and studied at the Jerusalem Conservatory of Music with Stefan Wolpe, Eli Friedmann, and Frank Pelleg. Further studies included work at Columbia University, New York. From 1955 to 1961, he conducted research concerning electroacoustics and electronic sound production in regard to their possibilities in the field of musical composition. After completing a lecture tour through the United States in 1962, he came to the University of Illinois one year later, primarily to do research on the significance of computer systems for composition. He is presently professor of music there.

Professor Brün participated in a variety of festivals and conferences: "Music of the Twentieth Century," Saarbrücken, Germany (May 1979, 1980, and 1981); "Composition Today," Munich, Germany (July 1982); American Society for Cybernetics Conferences (Columbus, Ohio, October 1982; Philadelphia, Pennsylvania, November 1984; and Virginia Beach, Virginia, February 1986); "Days of New Music," Bonn, Germany (June 1983); Digicon Conference, Vancouver, B.C. (August 1983, 1985); Gordon Research Conference on Cybernetics, New Hampton, New Hampshire (August 1984); Keynote Address at the International Computer Music Conference, Vancouver, B.C. (August 1985); and the Festival of American New Music, State University of New York at Buffalo (April 1986).

Professor Brün is on the editorial board of the *Computer Music Journal*. A record album of twelve of his compositions was released on the Non Sequitur label in 1983. Other compositions of his are available on the Opus One, CRI, and University of Illinois Experimental Music Studios labels.

KENNETH GABURO was born in 1926 and is internationally recognized for his innovative work, including one hundred and ten experimental compositions and numerous philosophical, aesthetic and sociopolitical writings. He founded the New Music Choral Ensemble in 1960, which performed two hundred new works; as well as *Lingua Press* in 1974, featuring one hundred and fifteen distinguished publications by seventy one authors. His honors have included grants from the Guggenheim foundation, UNESCO, Thorne, Fromm, Rockefeller, and Koussevitzky. In 1980 Dr. Gaburo staged the first uhrtext production of Harry Partch's *Bewitched* at the Berlin Festival. In 1984 his *Antiphony 7 (Revolution)* for one percussionist and tape received its premiere at California Institute of the Arts. He is presently professor of music at the University of Iowa.

About his work, he writes: "The inquiry of music-as-language, language-as-music, *(Compositional Linguistics)*, begun in 1953, has taken me to domains not otherwise possible, and not constrained by the assumed 'boundaries' of music. Instead, I view each work as *expressive language*, . . . a multidimensional structure . . . , in which physicality, theatrical space, and human presence are as vital as is 'sound.'"

ROBIN JULIAN HEIFETZ earned a doctorate in composition from the University of Illinois at Urbana-Champaign in 1978 where he studied with Sal Martirano and Herbert Brün. He has served as composer-in-residence at Stiftelsen EMS Stockholm, Sweden; Computer Music Studio, Colgate University, Hamilton, New York; Sonic Research Studios, Simon Fraser University, Burnaby, Canada; Electronic Music Studio, Tel-Aviv University, Israel; Instituut voor Psychoakustika en Electronische Muziek, Rijksuniversiteit-Gent, Belgium; and Audio-Digital Laboratories, Vancouver, Canada. From 1980 to 1984 he was a assistant professor and director of The Center for Experimental Music of The Hebrew University of Jerusalem, Israel; and from 1984 to 1986 he was an assistant professor and director of The Institute for the Musical Arts, Ramat Hanegev College, Yeroham, Israel.

Dr. Heifetz has won the 2° PRIX at the 7ème Concours International de Musique Electroacoustique de Bourges 1979, France; a 1980 National Endowment for the Arts Composer Fellowship (the work receiving its world premiere at Centre Georges Pompidou, Paris in 1983); Honorable Mentions at the 9ème Concours International de Musique Electroacoustique de Bourges 1981, and that same year at the 4° Concorso Internazionale "Luigi Russolo" di Musica Elettroacustica, Varese, Italy; and the 2nd Prizes at the 1st and 4th New England Computer Music Association's International Computer Music Competitions, Boston, in 1983 and 1986 respectively. His electroacoustic music is commercially recorded by Folkways; Orion; and L'Atelier Créatif de Musique Electro-Acoustique, Belgium. His articles have been published by *Interface: Journal of New Music Research*, *The Music Review*, and *Journal of Musicology*, among others. In 1983 he served as the technical advisor in electroacoustic music for Roger Kamien's *MUSIC: An Appreciation*, 3d ed., published by McGraw Hill; and since 1986 he has been a contributing editor of *The Journal of The Society for Electro-Acoustic Music in the U.S.*, and in 1987 he was the national secretary of that organization.

LEJAREN HILLER received his Ph.D. in chemistry in 1947 at Princeton University and his M.Mus. in 1958 at the University of Illinois, having already studied composition with Roger Sessions and Milton Babbitt at Princeton. He was a research chemist at E.I. du Pont de Nemours from 1947 to 1952 and from 1952 to 1958 was a member of the department of chemistry at the University of Illinois. From 1958 until 1968 he was a professor of music there, where he designed and built the University of Illinois Experimental Music Studio.

Since 1968 Dr. Hiller has been at the State University of New York at Buffalo, where he is currently the Birge-Cary Professor of Music. Until 1975 he was also codirector, with Lukas Foss, of the Buffalo Center of the Creative and Performing Arts. He is the author of three books and numerous articles on science, music, and the arts in general. He is the composer of some seventy two scores for instruments, voice, electronics, computer, film, theater, and television.

THOMAS E. JANZEN was born in Chicago in 1955 and began composing works with a wide variety of idioms and instruments in 1971. In 1977, he earned a B.A. in broadcasting from the California State University at Northridge, where he also continued his composition studies and made the outline for the essay included in this anthology. In 1984, he moved to Massachusetts and added performance art to his creative presentations, combining various media with synthesis and digital signal processing. Mr. Janzen has developed computer programs for sound synthesis and stochastic composition and has implemented Xenakis' Free Stochastic Music Program (published in the book, *Formalized Music*) under VAX VMS. He has built his own synthesizers as well as his own designs for sound synthesis and processing circuits. He presently finds employment designing hardware and software for logic IC testing in a large computer manufacturing firm.

LEONARD KASDAN is professor of social anthropology and resource and environmental studies at Dalhousie University in Halifax, Nova Scotia. He has carried out research in the Middle East, Scotland, and Atlantic Canada. His principal interests are in the areas of cultural and social change, particularly as they are affected by changes in technology and government policies.

DAVID KEANE's music is heard frequently in television, radio, stage drama, experimental projection, and film productions, and he has written several operas. He has received awards for his work in France, England, the United States, and Canada, and he has been awarded numerous commissions administered by the Ontario Arts Council as well as the Canada Council. He has also produced work for the National Film Board, the National Art Gallery of

Canada, the CBC, the National Design Council, and the Ontario Science Center. Outside Canada, Keane has received commissions from MAFILM (Hungary), G.M.E.B. (France), the National Endowment for the Arts (U.S.), and the Cuban Commission for UNESCO. His works have been heard recently at such major international festivals as Almeida (London), Bourges (France), Tokyo, Warsaw Autumn, Zagreb Biennial, and the ISCM World Music Days (Amsterdam), among many others. His music is frequently broadcast throughout North America and western and eastern Europe, and has been included on such regular concert series as EMAS (London), Fylkingen (Stockholm), Forum für Aktuelle Kunst (Innsbruck), GAMO (Florence), Musica Verticale (Rome), and the Palais des Beaux Arts (Brussels).

He is presently professor of theory and composition at Queen's University, Kingston, Ontario, and director of that institution's electroacoustic music studios, which he founded in 1970. He is widely known and respected as an author and lecturer on aspects of contemporary music and musical aesthetics. Since 1977 Professor Keane has toured extensively in Europe and North America, supervising performances of his compositions and lecturing. His music is available through Universal Edition (London) and the Canadian Music Centre. Disc recordings are available on the Music Gallery Editions and Cambridge Street Records labels.

OTTO LUENING was born in Milwaukee in 1900, and studied in Germany and Switzerland, notably with Philipp Jarnach and Ferruccio Busoni, while earning a living as a flutist. He then returned to the United States in 1920 to begin a career as composer, conductor, flutist and teacher at the Eastman School of Music, the University of Arizona, Bennington College, the Juilliard School of Music, Barnard College, and Columbia University. He has been active, often as chief officer, in the American Music Center, Composers Recordings, Inc., the American Academy in Rome, Yaddo, and the American Composers Alliance.

He is a life member of the American Academy and Institute of Arts and Letters and has received many other honors. He has some three hundred compositions to his credit. One of the pioneers in the development of electroacoustic music, he also conducted the world premieres of such landmark American operas as Virgil Thomson's *The Mother of Us All*, Gian Carlo Menotti's *The Medium*, and his own *Evangeline*. His autobiography, *The Odyssey of an American Composer*, was published in 1980 by Charles Scribner's Sons.

PRISCILLA MCLEAN was born in Fitchburg, Massachusetts in 1942, and received her M.M. in composition from Indiana University in 1969. She taught at St. Mary's College, Notre Dame, Indiana; Indiana University at Kokomo; and at the University of Hawaii at Manoa. Since 1976 she has become an internationally acclaimed composer and performer (with her husband Barton McLean as the McLean Mix) of electroacoustic music, performing over one hundred concerts in the U.S. and Europe.

She is also the director of MLC Publications, recipient of four National Endowment for the Arts grants since 1978 (among numerous other grants and awards), and a contributing reporter for *Musical America Magazine.* Six commercial recordings are available of her music. Her latest music incorporates sounds of the wilderness, and with electronics she is creating a unique genre that is drawing wide attention.

JOHN MELBY was born in 1941 in Whitehall, Wisconsin. He received his musical education at the Curtis Institute of Music (Dip. and B.Mus.), the University of Pennsylvania (M.A.), and Princeton University (M.F.A. and the Ph.D.). His composition teachers included Vincent Persichetti, Henry Weinberg, George Crumb, Peter Westergaard, J. K. Randall, and Milton Babbitt. His works, particularly those for computer-synthesized tape, both with and without live performers, have been performed all over the world and many of them have been commercially recorded. He is the recipient of many grants and awards, including a Guggenheim Fellowship and an award from the American Academy and Institute of Arts and Letters. Dr. Melby's music is published by Margun Music, Inc. and American Composers Edition and is recorded by Composers Recordings, Inc., New World Records, and Advance Records. He is presently a professor of composition and theory at the University of Illinois at Urbana-Champaign.

DEXTER MORRILL was born in North Adams, Massachusetts in 1938. He studied composition with William Skelton, Leonard Ratner, and Robert Palmer. During the 1960s, he was a Ford Foundation Young Composer Fellow in Universal City, Missouri. Since 1971, Dr. Morrill has been the director of the computer music studio at Colgate University, where he is professor of music. His computer music compositions have received performances in the United States, Canada, Australia, Great Britain, Poland, Czechoslovakia, and most western European countries. He was a guest researcher at IRCAM in 1980, a visiting professor of music at the State University of New York at Binghamton and Stanford University, and has spent a good part of his time doing research on the analysis and synthesis of trumpet tones. Professor Morrill has received composition grants from the National Endowment for the Arts and the New York State Arts Council, as well as numerous other commissions. He has written a book on computer music instruments for the Kaufmann Press and was commissioned to compose a work for trumpeter Wynton Marsalis in 1988. His works are available on the Golden Crest, Musical Heritage, and Redwood labels.

JAN W. MORTHENSON was born in 1940 and presently lives in Stockholm, where he is active as a composer and lecturer and affiliated with Stiftelsen Elektro-akustisk Musik i Sverige. He has published two books: *Non-figurative Music* (German edition, 1966) and *Foundations of Composition* (Swedish edition, 1986). He is a former vice president of the International Society for Contemporary Music and is currently involved in the production of experimental television works.

BARRY SCHRADER has distinguished himself in several areas of contemporary music. His compositions, which are primarily in the field of electroacoustic music, have been performed throughout the world and are commercially available on the Opus One and Laurel Record labels and on Modern Visual Communication video. He has composed live/electronic and computer music as well as works for dance, theater, multimedia, film, television, and video.

He is also a teacher, author, and lecturer on various aspects of electroacoustic music and is widely known for his book, *Introduction to Electro-Acoustic Music,* and his contributions to the *Grove Dictionary of American Music.* Active in the areas of concert and organizational activities, Schrader was a founding member of the Southern California Resource for Electro-Acoustic Music and the Society for Electro-Acoustic Music in the United States, serving as that organization's first president. Since 1971, he has been on the composition faculty of California Institute of the Arts, where he is presently the artistic director of the electroacoustic music studios.

DARIA SEMEGEN studied at the Eastman School of Music, Yale and Columbia Universities, and in Warsaw, Poland as a Fulbright scholar. She is a composer of instrumental, vocal, and electroacoustic music and has received numerous awards in composition. She has been on the teaching staff of the Columbia-Princeton Electronic Music Center and since 1974 has been a member of the music faculty at the State University of New York at Stony Brook, where she is associate professor and a director of the electronic music studios.